Admiral Togo and the Imperial Navy at War

Admiral Togo and the Imperial Navy at War

Two Accounts of the Rise of Japanese Sea Power and Its Finest Commander

ILLUSTRATED

Admiral Togo
Arthur Lloyd

The Naval Battles of the Russo-Japanese War
Kichitaro Togo

LEONAUR

Admiral Togo and the Imperial Navy at War
Two Accounts of the Rise of Japanese Sea Power and Its Finest Commander
Admiral Togo
by Arthur Lloyd
The Naval Battles of the Russo-Japanese War
by Kichitaro Togo

ILLUSTRATED

FIRST EDITION

First published under the titles
Admiral Togo
and
The Naval Battles of the Russo-Japanese War

Leonaur is an imprint of Oakpast Ltd

Copyright in this form © 2017 Oakpast Ltd

ISBN: 978-1-78282-646-0 (hardcover)
ISBN: 978-1-78282-647-7 (softcover)

http://www.leonaur.com

Contents

Admiral Togo

Contents

Preface

For the imperfections of the present volume I can only plead that I hope it may prove to be a first edition, and that further studies and the publication of more detailed information may enable me at some future time to complete, or at least to elaborate, the biography of a great man in whom the whole world is interested.

The modest and retiring life which Admiral Togo has hitherto lived has made it difficult for the biographer to collect many picturesque incidents relating to his early years. But modesty is one of the greatest of virtues, and that he has always exhibited this virtue in so conspicuous a manner seems to be one of the elements which make the greatness of his character.

Arthur Lloyd.

Tokyo. August, 1905.

Madame Tetsuko Togo

CHAPTER 1

The Beginnings of Japan's Naval History

If we were writing an account of the naval history of Great Britain, we should probably choose as our starting-point the history of the Spanish Armada and its signal overthrow in the sixteenth century.

This choice of a starting point would not imply that there is to be found no sea-fighting in English records of an earlier date. An island-kingdom like England must always have been both vulnerable and defensible along her coastlines and harbours, and Englishmen have all through their history been fighters on the sea. But the Spanish Armada first demonstrated to Englishmen the prime importance of a standing fleet as a permanent wall of defence, and the creation of the British Navy was the logical outcome of the defence hastily organised against the fleets of Spain, in spite of the fact that the civil troubles, which, in England, followed so soon after the destruction of the *Armada*, interposed some years between the recognition of the need and the creation of the navy.

Japan, a sea-girt land, had a warning of possible danger from its invasion by sea many years before England received hers, and though the civil troubles which supervened in Japan were of far longer duration than those in England, and though Japan had to wait in consequence much longer than did England, before she became a naval Power, yet the logical birthday of the Japanese Navy was so very much like the birthday of the British naval Power that I cannot help commencing my book with it.

The British Navy was practically born when the Lord High Admiral of Queen Elizabeth was commanded to equip a fleet as best he could to repel the threatened invasion of the Spaniards. The Japanese

Navy may also be said to have been born when Hojo Tokimune the Regent, in 1275, took his measures for repelling the Mongolian invasion.

Kublai Khan, the great Mongolian leader of the Middle Ages, had succeeded in overthrowing the Sung Dynasty in China and making himself master of the whole of the Celestial Empire. He had further reduced to submission the entire peninsula of Korea, and having reached the extreme limits of the Asiatic mainland, began to cast covetous eyes towards the beautiful and happily-situated islands which form a defensive barrier for the eastern shores of that Continent.

Koppitsuretsu (to give him his Japanese name, Kublai Khan being the name by which Europeans know him better through the writings of the famous Venetian, Marco Polo),—Koppitsuretsu doubtless thought that Japan would be an easy prey for his armies. There was every reason to make him think so.

Never was a country more extraordinarily governed, or misgoverned, than Japan in the thirteenth century. A series of long intrigues within the court brought about a succession of abdications, forced or voluntary, which frequently left the occupant of the throne a mere shadow of Imperial dignity. The actual functions of the executive were in the hands of a Shogun, who was supposed to act in all things as the emperor's representative; but similar intrigues in the entourage of the Shogun reduced this high functionary to a mere "puppet" in the hands of his retainers, one of whom, residing at Kamakura, acted as his representative, with the title of "Regent."

Western readers will scarce believe me when I say that, in the Hojo family, a custom arose of having nominal "regents" as well, but they will not be astonished to be told that, under this extraordinary system of carrying on affairs of state, the whole country was in anarchy and confusion, and everyone did practically what was good in his eyes. The Buddhist priests reaped a temporary harvest of wealth and influence from the system, which was one of their own creating, but even in the ranks of the priesthood voices were raised against the misgovernment of the times, and the life of Nichiren, the most picturesque of Buddhist reformers, is full of the troubles which his vigorous protests brought upon him.

Under these circumstances, we cannot wonder that Kublai Khan, elated with his conquests la Korea and China, should have fallen into the error of under-estimating the pride and strength of the Japanese people. He wrote a letter couched in insolent terms, to the reigning

Emperor (Go-Uda Tenno 1257—1287), demanding submission and tribute from the Empire of Japan, but his insolence overshot the mark. The Regent of the time, Hojo Tokimune, though quite a young man, was proud and high spirited, and had no hesitation as to the course to be adopted. He sent the Korean envoys of the Mongolian conqueror back to China with scornful words, which he showed to be deliberately chosen by repeating them to a second embassy sent in the following year.

Kublai Khan was too great a potentate, and had been too openly defied, to sit down tamely under the insults of the Japanese. He collected an army in Korea which he embarked on board a fleet of 450 Korean war *junks*, seized the islands of Iki and Tsushima, which have played so great a role in the present war against Russia, and landed on the coasts of Kyushu, where he was, however, repulsed by the Japanese, after desperate fighting. This was in 1275: three years later Kublai Khan sent another ambassador, and yet another, to Japan, urging the Island Empire to submit and send him tribute; but Tokimune beheaded them both.

The result was that Kublai Khan, deeply insulted, vowed a tremendous vengeance against the insolent islanders, and prepared armies and fleets far greater than those he had sent before. It was a critical moment for Japan. The people were moved with a mixture of anger and apprehension; Nichiren preached and wrote, exhorting, reproving, and urging much-needed social reforms; the emperor went in state to the Temples at Ise to pray to his ancestress, Amaterasu, goddess of the sun, for help against the enemies of the country; Tokimune talked little but collected an army and went forth to battle.

The Mongols had landed and were encamped near Takashima, where Tokimune attacked them, and, after desperate fighting, drove them back to their ships. Then came an interposition of the Divine Providence which has so frequently manifested itself in the affairs of Japan. Scarcely had the Mongol troops found refuge on board their ships when a terrible storm arose and destroyed their whole fleet (*A.D.* 1281).

Many readers have seen the obvious parallel between the Mongol Invasion of Japan and the Spanish Armada. Many have also seen the obvious similarity between the Mongolian Invasion and the Russian Expedition from the Baltic. This is not the case to discuss these similarities. What I wish to say here is that as the Spanish Armada had its logical outcome in the creation of a standing navy, so the logical outcome of the Mongol Invasion was the Navy of Japan to-day.

In each country, a threatened invasion demonstrated the absolute importance of a navy as a first line of defence. In England, where the internal troubles were fortunately of short duration, little more than fifty years elapsed before the fleets of the Commonwealth were busy defending the interests of England against the navies of France and the Dutch Republic. In Japan where the evils of state and society were far more deep-seated, and where the civil dissensions, followed by the iron repression of all activity by the Tokugawas, lasted for well-nigh six hundred years, the logical outcome of that lesson was correspondingly long in being realised.

But assuredly the lesson was given in Japan as well as in England. If Providence interposed in the two cases to work signal deliverance, it was not to encourage either nation to a blind trust in Providence in the future. God helps those that help themselves, and the obvious lesson which both nations were meant to learn, and have learned, is that island-empires need floating-walls to protect them.

For the practical realisation of the Japanese Navy we must jump over a period of six hundred years from the Mongol Invasion to the middle of the nineteenth century when the day was rapidly coming for Japan to come out of her seclusion to play a part in the world worthy of her dignity and providential mission. We call it her providential mission, because if the hand of Providence was clearly to be seen in the wonderful deliverance from the Mongols, the thoughtful student may also see the traces of the same hand in the seclusion from the world which followed the establishment of the Tokugawas, (a seclusion the maintenance of which was little less than marvellous) and the timely emergence of the nation, as of a people born in a day, to bring a new element of life and vigour into a civilization which was beginning to suffer from senility and decay.

The nineteenth century made it impossible to maintain any longer the seclusion of Japan. The trade of Europe was expanding, the civilization of America had emerged on the Pacific coast, Australia had been discovered, steam was revolutionizing navigation. From all sides ships came past the coasts of Japan, some desirous of traffic, some for water and help, some to restore castaway Japanese fisherman. Intercourse became unavoidable, and many of the patriotic Japanese feared that intercourse would mean the loss of national independence.

Amongst those who felt much anxiety on this subject was Prince Shimazu, lord of Satsuma, one of the most powerful of Japanese Princes, and one whose territories, situated in the extreme South and West of Japan proper, gave him much cause for anxiety on this subject, Satsuma was by no means the only baron who felt anxiety on this point. The lords of Mito and Tosa, nay, even the Shogunal Cabinet itself were much exercised about it, and at last in the year 1847, after much deliberation and debate, a resolution was come to by the *Shogunate*, not only to undertake the work of Naval Organisation itself, but to allow the great territorial nobles, who ruled as kings within their own dominions, to raise squadrons for the defence of the seaboard of Japan.

The Prince of Satsuma was one of the first of the Daimyos to avail himself of this permission. The Satsuma Fleet was soon one of the most powerful of the local fleets. We shall find the prince petitioning the Central Government in 1853 for permission to build not merely small vessels for coast-defence, but large ships capable of keeping the sea and pursuing a retreating enemy. We shall find him later on sending up to the North a Fleet capable of engaging the Shogunal Navy under Enomoto, which was making its last stand at Hakodate.

We shall also see the Satsuma Fleet emerging victorious from these engagements and so becoming, in the new era which dawned upon Japan after the war of the Restoration, the nucleus of the present Imperial Navy of Japan Admiral Togo's first sea-service was in the Satsuma Navy: his subsequent career has been with the Imperial Navy from its very commencement.

This history of his life is therefore very much a history of the Imperial Navy of Japan, with which he has been so long and so constantly identified. But, before writing it, it will be well to devote one more preliminary chapter to the consideration of the *Satsuma Daimyate* which has furnished so many of the best men to the services of the Japanese Empire.

CHAPTER 2

Satsuma

The ancient Daimyate of Satsuma, ruled over by princes of the Shimazu family, occupied the southern portion of the Island of Kyushu, *i.e.* the whole of the provinces of Satsuma and Osumi, together with portions of Hyuga, and several islands off the coast. The Lord of Satsuma was also in a sense a *suzerain* of the Loochoo Archipelago, for the ruler of those islands acknowledged a double dependence, and sent tribute not only to China but also to Satsuma.

The Satsuma Daimyos had always been very powerful, and their overlordship had extended itself on various occasions over the greater part of the island of Kyushu. They had also been for long years practically' independent of the Central Government in the days before the Tokugawa regime, and when, after the pacification which followed the Battle of Sekigahara, Shimazu was obliged to bow his head before Iyeyasu, he had done it with a bad grace and a reluctant heart. The Satsuma people had always resented the Tokugawa supremacy, and, living as they did in a very remote corner of the Empire, had always contrived to have a tolerably free hand in the management of their own affairs.

The Satsuma *samurai* were always noted for their poverty. their numbers were far greater, proportionately to other *daimyates*, in Satsuma than elsewhere, and the provision of rice, which it was the custom for all *daimyos* to give for the support of their retainers, was constantly, in Satsuma, insufficient for the support of the whole body of *samurai*. The *samurai* of this province, therefore, came in time to be distinguished from those of other provinces by their industry and thrift. They were obliged to work as farmers to eke out their allowances, they were obliged also to exercise the most rigid economy in the management of their households. They became, therefore, a sturdy

18

race not unlike the English yeomen of the middle ages, frugal, active, and independent, and whilst the *samurai* of other, more wealthy, *daimyate* were all succumbing more or less to the enervating influences of ease and freedom from pecuniary cares, the Satsuma men, like the Spartans in Greece, stood out conspicuously among their compatriots for simplicity, hardihood and practical common sense.

The country round Kagoshima, the capital of Satsuma, is admirable training ground for soldiers, and the Satsuma *samurai* were constantly, even in times of peace, kept at work with military manoeuvres and exercises of various kinds. Hence the Satsuma armies had always been vigorous and hard to beat, though the same might be said if the local armies maintained by many of the Japanese princes. East or West, North or South, the Japanese has always shown himself to be an excellent fighter.

But Satsuma, owing to its geographical position and political circumstances, had one advantage over all other *daimyates*. It had a long and dangerous seacoast, a deep, protected, bay whose calm waters afforded excellent opportunities for nautical training, and its prince was one of the overlords of Loochoo, a position which necessitated maritime journeys such as fell to the lot of the subjects of no other *daimyate*.

Thus, even in the Tokugawa days, when all commerce by sea was forbidden, the Satsuma people were a sea-faring folk.

The spirit which animated the Satsuma *samurai* may be seen from the following account which is given of the training of the young Kagoshima retainers.

Every village in the province had its own *Gochu* or village association of young men, and every young *samurai* was enrolled a member as soon as he reached the age of 14 or 15. The object of the *Gochu* was to encourage bravery, and the power of endurance, and its members were constantly being tested by their seniors and associates with a view to ascertaining their qualifications in this respect.

If a young man, on being tested, showed signs of fear; he received a warning from the senior members. If, on his next trial, he did better, he was forgiven and nothing more was said. If he "funked" again, however, then woe betide him. He was cut off from the society of young men, and no sentence of excommunication could possibly be worse than such exclusion.

Every member of a *Gochu* had to study for eight hours a day, four morning hours being devoted to "books," and four in the afternoon to practical exercises. On the 1st, 6th, 11th, 16th, 21st, and 26th of every month they practised writing, the 5th, 10th, 15th, 20th, 25th, and 30th were given to the reading of books on military subjects, the remaining days were in like manner devoted to subjects likely to be of practical use in the training of warrior caste. They had not many subjects and no useless ones, the few they had were thoroughly practical, and thoroughly well learned. Any neglect or violation of the rules of study was at once punished by the *Gochu*. We can see the traces of this custom still in the way in which members of the old *samurai* caste will throw themselves into the study of some special branch of practical science.

The *Gochu* had certain festivals of their own, not religious but patriotic, for patriotism with them took the place of religion. The Revenge of the Soga Brothers, and the tragic death of the Forty Seven Ronins, two of the most famous vendetta stories of mediaeval Japan, were celebrated with simple but appropriate ceremonies, the one on May 18, and the other on December 14. On these occasions the accounts of these heroes of olden times, and their deeds were represented in song and mime, and their youthful hearts were moved to compassion or admiration as the different scenes of the tragedies fell on their ears. Thus, we can imagine a gathering of Jewish lads to have been moved by the narrated prowess of Jephthah, Gideon, or David, or a class of Athenians roused to anger or melted to tears over the Iliad or the Odyssey. It is the story of men of one's own blood that appeals most strongly to the human heart.

It has been noted that the Shimazus needed no strongly fortified castle to keep their retainers in subjection. Contented and loyal subjects are the best possible bulwarks of a throne, and such were the retainers who surrounded the Lords of Satsuma.

We can understand now the moral atmosphere in which our hero was born and educated. Simple living, stern discipline, high thinking, if withal, somewhat narrow. In the moral and political regeneration of Japan, Satsuma (allied to Choshu and one or two other *daimyates*) played the part which Prussia did in Germany, or Sardinia in Italy. the *Shogunate*, like Austria in the one case, or Pio Nono in the other, clung loyally but blindly to a lost cause trying in vain to bolster up a political system which had outlived its day and become a hindrance to the healthy growth of the nation.

The motives were of the highest order, the patriotism of the defenders of these lost causes was in every case most admirable, but the causes were lost from the beginning, and their defenders were overwhelmed in the fall of the ramparts behind which they stood. Like Prussia, the men of Satsuma saw beforehand the crash that was inevitably coming, and took their measures to champion the true political creed on which alone Japan's greatness could be based.

The overthrow of the *Shogunate* and the restoration of the executive power to its proper possessor were both measures of inevitable necessity, and if from their timely advocacy of these measures the men of Satsuma and Choshu "sucked to themselves no small advantage," still the advantages to Japan as a whole have been still greater, and no fair-minded critic will be disposed to grudge them their position of honour in the councils and enterprises of the nation. *Palmam qui meruit ferat.*

CHAPTER 3

Togo's Birth and Early Education

Togo Heihachiro was born in Kajiya-machi, the *Samurai* quarter of Kagoshima, on the 22nd of December, 1847.

His family was descended from the ancient family of the Taira, which played so great a part in the Middle Ages of Japan. The last and, indeed, the only sage of the Taira family, Taira no Shigemori, had an only daughter, who, on the ruin of her house, being pursued by her enemy, the head of the rival Minamoto family, found an asylum in the territories of the Prince of Satsuma. Here she remained, educating her children, who, growing up, entered the service of the Satsuma Daimyo and were granted the surname of Togo.

It is said that this remote ancestress of the Togo house had, for reasons probably connected with the circumstances of her escape from the Minamoto, an aversion to riding on a white horse, and this tradition is said still to remain of force in the Togo family in the garden attached to the old family homestead in Kagoshima, now unfortunately destroyed by fire, there stood during Togo's boyhood a small shrine sacred to the memory of the first ancestress of the family.

The future admiral's father, Togo Kichizaemon, had a great reputation for probity and justice. He held the responsible office of *Kori Bugyo* or District Magistrate—an office not unlike the honourable post of Justice of the Peace which is the pride of many a country gentleman in England,—and discharged his difficult duties so well, that, at the request of his fellow-townsmen, he continued to hold it for thirteen consecutive years, though the usual period of tenure is only for three.

His character was very much like that of his illustrious son—simple, straightforward, somewhat taciturn, but kind and sincere. He was not a diplomat) but there was something statesmanlike about his straight-forward simplicity.

His mother, Masu-ko, is said to have been a fine-looking refined lady, the very type of woman that Kaibara Ekiken, the author of the celebrated *Onna-daigaku* (*Great learning for Women*), would have delighted to describe. She was frugal and orderly, an excellent housekeeper, and moreover, a splendid disciplinarian. She trained her children as a Spartan mother would have done, and was a convinced believer in the old saying about the devil and the idle hands.

She constantly kept her children busy with their studies and military exercises, and allowed them very little leisure in which to get into mischief. She had four sons, of whom Heihachiro was the third. The admiral's three brothers all took part in the rebellion of the elder Saigo, and perished at the Battle of Shiroyama. Fortunately for Heihachiro he was studying in England at the time, and out of reach of temptation.

In due course of time, Heihachiro, like the other lads of Kagoshima, entered a *Gochu*. The *Gochu* into which it was his good fortune to enter was one with an exceedingly good record. The elder Saigo, the flower of Japanese chivalry, had once been in its ranks: and one of Togo's boy companions and contemporaries was Kuroki, destined like himself to win distinction in war with the Russians.

One of Saigo's younger brothers was Togo's teacher of Chinese, and read the *Confucian Analects* with him. It was Togo's habit to rise early, before sunrise, and to stand at his teacher's gate till six o'clock, when he was permitted to enter and receive a lesson of two hours' duration. From eight o'clock till noon he was busy reviewing the lessons he had learned with his teacher, and the afternoon was spent, sometimes in study and sometimes in fencing and wrestling with Kuroki and other companions by the riverside.

As a boy, he was always noted for his quiet peaceable disposition. He very seldom concerned himself in the quarrels which took place between the different *Gochu* in the city, and rarely had any quarrels of his own on hand. Yet he always contrived to hold his own amongst his comrades, who deferred to him as boys do to one in whom they see a capacity for leadership, even though he takes no step to assert himself, or to lord it over his comrades.

In 1863, at the age of seventeen, Togo entered the Satsuma Navy, as a cadet. It has been said that the real cause of the establishment of that Navy was fear of Russia, whose aggressions were even then known and dreaded by Japanese Statesmen. We have also heard it maintained that when, shortly after the Imperial Restoration, the elder Saigo was led astray into rebellious paths, his moving reason was not a dissatisfaction at the comparatively small amount of recognition given to Satsuma in the Imperial Councils, but a desire to see a more resolute policy against Russia adopted by Japan, together with a resolution to get the power into his own hands, so as the better to prosecute a line of policy which he felt to be of vital importance to his country.

Be that as it may, the first foreign enemy to be encountered by Japanese armies was not Russia, but England. The discontent with which patriotic Japanese saw the sacred soil of their country defiled by foreign feet, together with the growing lawlessness of the times, made it impossible for the authorities, national or consular, to avoid all disturbances between Japanese and foreigners. Outrages against the barbarians were of frequent occurrence: attacks were made upon the British Legation in Yedo, ships passing through the Straits of Shimonoseki were fired on by the fortresses of the Prince of Choshu, and one incident in particular occurred, which brought Satsuma, individually, into trouble with the English authorities.

A troop of Satsuma retainers who were accompanying the uncle of their prince on his way to Yedo, on the 14th of September 1862, attacked a party of foreigners riding peaceably along the high road near Kanagawa, and murdered one of them, an Englishman named Richardson. The British authorities promptly demanded satisfaction from the *Shogunate*, but, whilst getting an indemnity from the Yedo Government, were referred for full satisfaction to the Prince of Satsuma, as the feudal lord of the men who had made the attack, and as being, therefore, a responsible party in the affair. Satsuma, white deeply regretting the incident at Namamugi (the hamlet at which the attack was made), and willing to pay a money indemnity for the thoughtless act of his turbulent retainers, absolutely refused to hand over the perpetrators of the crime to the English, as they desired.

Some delay occurred over the negotiations, but at last, in August 1863, an English Squadron arrived in the Bay of Kagoshima, and, failing to get its demands satisfied, proceeded to bombard the town. The engagement took place on the 15th August 1863. The Kagoshima authorities were much surprised by a visit which they hardly expected. They were still more taken aback, when the English summoned three vessels belonging to the Satsuma Navy, which they found at anchor in a remote corner of the bay, to shift their anchorage, and take up a new position in the midst of the British Squadron, an order which the

The Bombardment of Kagoshima

Japanese vessels obeyed without apparently knowing what it meant.

This action the Japanese claim to have been a treacherous one on the part of the British; but the British, on their part, thought they had just cause for complaint, when, at the stroke of noon, without any previous warning, the Kagoshima forts opened fire on their unwelcome visitors.

A fierce cannonading then ensued, which did much damage without leading to any very tangible results. The weather was boisterous and stormy so that the British could not have landed a party of men even if they had had the force requisite for the operation. They burned the three Satsuma vessels and reduced a large portion of the town to ashes, but without silencing the forts.

On the other hand, they suffered severely themselves: one of their ships went ashore and only got off with the loss of her anchor, which was afterwards restored by the Japanese; and there were many losses both of officers and men. The next morning, they sailed out of the bay, to avoid a threatening typhoon, leaving behind them an indecisive record. They had reduced the city to ashes and destroyed a part of the fleet of Satsuma; but the forts were never silenced, and they sailed away without having got their demands. The indemnity was paid in September 1863, but the Satsuma authorities never surrendered the persons of Richardson's murderers.

The bombardment of Kagoshima was Togo Heihachiro's baptism of fire, and Japanese writers tell us, with great pride, how the future admiral, stripped to the skin, was working at the guns in one of the batteries on that eventful day.

It is worthy of note that on this day the Japanese fired the first shot, without waiting for any formal declaration of hostilities. We remember as we write down the fact that it was Togo as captain of the *Naniwa*, who sunk the *Kaosheng* in the war with China, and Togo who, as admiral, ordered the discharge of the first torpedo against the Russian vessels at Port Arthur.

In neither case had hostilities been declared when the first shot was fired. Can it have been Togo who applied the fuse to the first gun fired at Kagoshima? The Satsuma Navy covered itself with glory in this action. It had held its own in a fair fight with a British Squadron, and had lost nothing except the three steamers which had been taken by surprise, and placed as it were *hors de combat* before the action commenced.

But the bombardment had the effect of arousing the whole nation

1, Batchrsa. — 2. Peudy. — 3. Coquette. — 4. Perseus. — 5. Argus. — 6. Euryalus. — 7. Batteries japonaises. — A. 3 steamers japonais incendiés. — B. Jonque japonaise incendiée.
G. Palais. — D. Fonderies.

EXPÉDITION DU JAPON. — Bombardement de Kagosima par la flotte anglaise. (D'après un croquis de M. Barbier.)

to the need of naval armaments. The Shogunate, Satsuma, Choshu, and perhaps one or two more *daimyates* had hitherto been the only ones that paid any attention to coast defence, but now the whole nation was roused to action. Even the emperor bestirred himself and bade his subjects "sweep the *Kurofune* (black ships) off the sea."

★★★★★★

I have seen a poem by Komei Tenno, the father of the present emperor, which runs somewhat like this:

Perish my body in the cold clear depth
Of some dark well, but let no foreign foot
Pollute that water with its presence here.

★★★★★★

Many small navies made their appearance in different provinces, but none could compete with the Navy of Satsuma which had been in action with foreigners, and, had passed safely through the ordeal. The Choshu ships did not come out so well in their conflict with the foreign vessels at Shimonoseki. But then Choshu's glory has always been great in the army.

The next few years were uneventful years in the history of the Satsuma Navy: years of preparation for great events generally are. Nothing much is known of our hero during this period, except that he continued to serve with diligence in his profession, and that he gained a reputation as an excellent officer, silent and unobtrusive, but quick in decision and decisive in action.

It was evident that the Revolution which was to put the *Mikado* in his proper position, and place the men of the South on the top of those of the North, was coming on at a rapid pace, and Togo must often have heard, and perhaps sung, the verses in which San-yo Rai describes the Satsuma *Bushi*.

1. Short are our skirts—down to the knees: and short our sleeves—just to the elbow.

2, At our hips are our swords that can cut through iron.

3. If horse touch them or man touch them, they will kill him at once.

4. The youth of eighteen enters the Society of the strong Youths.

5. If a visitor comes from the North, with what shall we entertain him?

6. Bullets and powder shall be the tables and dishes.

7. And if, perchance, the visitor should not relish them.
8. The sword over his head shall give a closing dish.

★★★★★★

> Koromo wa kan ni itari, sode wan ni itaru :
> Yōkan no shūsui tetsu tatsubeshi;
> Hito furureba, hito wo kiri, uma furureba uma wo kiru.
> Jūhachi majiwari wo musubu, kenji no sha :
> Hokkaku yoku kitaraba, nani wo motte ka mukuin ?
> Dangwan shōyaku kore zenshu :
> Kaku·moshi shoku-en sezumba,
> Yoshi hōtō wo motte kare ga kōbe ni kuwaen.

★★★★★★

CHAPTER 4

The Civil War at the Time of the Restoration: 1867–1869

We next find Togo at Kyoto in the year 1867. Satsuma and Choshu men had made good their claim to be the protectors of the Imperial person, and driving out from Kyoto the rival Tokugawa clans, and the men of Hikone and Aizu, had occupied that city in force. The Shogunate Government, general known as the Bakufu, had been abolished, and an Imperial Government at Kyoto proclaimed in its stead.

The Tokugawa party were thoroughly discontented. Riots broke out in Yedo which the Shogunal police were unable to quell. The *Satsuma-yashiki* at Mita was burnt to the ground, and the Satsuma adherents in the stronghold of the Tokugawas escaped with difficulty to Shinagawa, where they were taken on board a small vessel, the *Kosho Maru*. One of the Shogunate war-ships, the *Kwaiten Maru*, commanded by Enomoto Kamajiro, went in pursuit, and after a desperate fight, in which the crew of the *Kosho* plugged the shot-holes in the hull with their own clothes, succeeded in doing her so much damage that the Satsuma men were obliged to abandon her, and only managed to join their own men at Kyoto with great difficulty.

When the Shogun heard of the troubles in Yedo and the burning of the *Satsuma-yashiki*, he at once petitioned the emperor for permission to chastise the men of Satsuma, and then, without waiting for a permission which he had very little chance of getting, marched from Osaka, where he was staying in the Great Castle of the Tokugawas, with all his forces for Kyoto. But the men of the "Four Loyal Clans," Satsuma, Choshu, Tosa and Higo, marched out to meet him, a battle was fought at Fushimi (28 January 1868), and the *shogun*, defeated and a fugitive, appeared at Hyogo, where he was taken on board an

American man of-war, which afterwards transferred him to the *Kaiyo Maru*, one of his own vessels. This ship, of which Enomoto was made captain, conveyed the *shogun* to Yedo.;

When the *Kaiyo Maru* had been coming down from Shinagawa to Osaka and Hyogo, to look after the interests of the *shogun*, she had met two Satsuma transports carrying troops from Kagoshima for garrison duty in Kyoto, and had fired on them as they left that port. This was before the Battle of Fushimi. The transports at once returned to port and gave information. A protest followed, but the *Shogunal* authorities justified the action of the *Kaiyo Maru* in firing on the transports. Satsuma and Yedo were practically at war, they said, and there had already been some fighting off Shinagawa.

The Satsuma men were obliged, therefore, to take measures of self-defence. They had no ships of war with them, but the *Kasuga Maru* was lying off Kobe, out of commission, it is true, but still available for convoy service, if she could be fitted out.

This was done with all speed: the ship was hastily prepared for sea, and manned from the troops brought up by the transports. The Satsuma garrison in Kyoto was able to furnish the officers. Akatsuka Genroku was appointed captain, Ito Sukemaro (the elder brother of the admiral) vice-captain, and Togo Heihachiro one of the junior lieutenants.

As soon as the ship was fitted out she was brought round to Osaka, The *shogun's* ship was not to be seen, so the transports started on their journey to Kagoshima, with the *Kasuga Maru* to convoy them. Presently, off the coast of Awa, the *Kaiyo Maru* was seen coming through the clearing mist, close to them: and the *Kasuga Maru*, in spite of her imperfect equipment and scratch crew, at once engaged her. The fight lasted for some time, without any very serious loss on either side, then, suddenly, the *Kaiyo Maru* sheered off and returned to port, and the *Kasuga Maru* hastened on to look after her transports, which had now reached a place of comparative safety.

This engagement took place on the 3rd day of the 1st month (old style) of the year 1868. Togo distinguished himself by his activity in helping to get the crew together and the ship ready for action, as also by his coolness under fire. His superiors saw him to be a steady man on whom they might rely,—and these are the men who succeed in making a name for themselves. The action was not a very great one, but it gave the Satsuma men an opportunity of proving their metal, and in the action Togo did his duty.

The Civil War had now broken out, and the Tokugawa party found one of its staunchest supporters in Enomoto, whom we have already seen as captain of the *Kaiyo*, but who will now appear as the admiral in command of the *Shogunal* Fleets.

The victory at Fushimi was only the first of a series of successful actions, which gradually brought the whole island under the rule of the emperor and his forces, and during the summer of 1863, the *shogun* was ordered to deliver to the emperor the Castle of Yedo, and all his forces military and naval. To this order, the *shogun* complied as far as he could, but his retainers were far more active in his support than he was himself, and Admiral Enomoto, on receiving the order to surrender his ships, quietly sailed out of Shinagawa Bay, with 11 ships, at early dawn on Aug. 22 1868, and took himself north to Hakodate, where some of the northern *daimyos* were still under arms for the lost cause of the *Shogunate*.

A landing was made at Hakodate, the loyalist *daimyo* of Matsumae was defeated at Esashi, a temporary government was established, and measures taken for a prolonged resistance. Enomoto's fleet was a factor of prime importance. He had eleven ships in all: his opponent had only four or five; and, with Hakodate as his base of operations, he might be a terrible thorn in the side of the newly restored Imperial Government.

The Imperial Government at once took action to crush the Hakodate scheme, A force of 6500 troops was hastily despatched north, together with a squadron under the command of Akatsuka, whom we have already seen as captain of the *Kasuga Maru*. Togo was still serving on board the *Kasuga*, which was now in better trim than it had been for the hastily planned engagement off the coast of Awa, and the Loyalist Fleet was strengthened by the addition of a new iron-clad war vessel, the *Stonewall Jackson*, recently purchased from the American Government by the *shogun's* government, and waiting in Yokohama to be delivered. Since giving the order, the *shogun's* government had collapsed, and there being apparently no other person authorised to take delivery, the American minister at last consented to have it transferred to the Imperial Government.

The squadron, thus strengthened, left Shinagawa on March the 9th, and on the 24th March, was at Kuwagasaki, a point not far from Hakodate. Here a fight took place, on April 29, The *Shogunal* Flagship, *Kwaiten*, with two other vessels, attempted a surprise attack on the Loyalists which was nearly successful. Most of the Loyalist captains

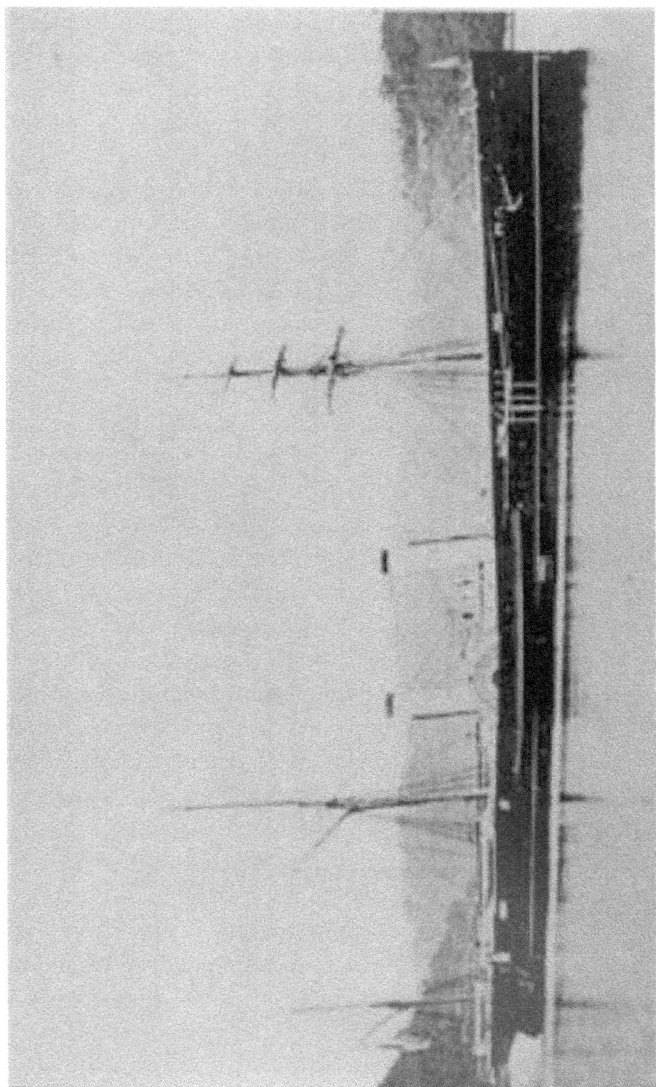

The Kasuga

were ashore at the time when the attack was made, but the fog caused the *Shogunal* vessels to part company, and the *Kwaiten* alone arrived at the place of destination. Here she found the *Stonewall Jackson*, now known as the *Musashi*, lying at anchor, and expecting nothing less than an attack from the *shogun's* forces. The *Musashi*, was an iron-clad, but that consideration did not prevent the *Kwaiten* from proceeding to the attack, and she manoeuvred so skilfully that presently the two ships were lying alongside of one another, and the rebels, leaping on board the *Musashi*, tried to capture her by assault. The attempt failed, however, and the *Kwaiten* had considerable difficulty in extricating herself from the dangerous position into which her daring had placed her.

Meanwhile her two consorts, the *Banryu* and *Takao*, which had lost her in the fog, seeing that the attack had failed, did their best to return to Hakodate. In this the *Banryu* succeeded, but the *Takao*, pursued by the *Kasuga* (Togo's ship) ran aground near Omotomura and was fired by her own crew.

The engagement at Kumagasaki did much to restore the balance between the two fleets. The Imperialists had, it is true, lost over 100 men while the Rebel loss was only 17 killed and 34 wounded; but they had lost one of their best ships, the *Takao*, and as the *Kwaiyo*, which we have already seen in action off Awa, had been lost during a gale, the *Shogunal* Fleet was now not much stronger than the Loyalist, and had no vessel that could withstand the iron-clad *Musashi*.

The remnants of Enomoto's Fleet were soon after this completely disposed of. In May 1869, the Imperialist ships were engaged in the task of covering the landing of troops on the shores of Yezo near Esashi, and the rebels, after vainly attempting to defend that town, were at last driven back into Hakodate, which was invested. During these operations, the *shogun's* people lost all their smaller ships, so that, by the end of the month, they were reduced to three ships, *Kwaiten*, *Banryu* and *Chiyoda*, all three of which had been more or less damaged in action.

On the 14th June, the *Chiyoda* struck on a rock and was abandoned by her crew. The next morning, she floated off without assistance, and came floating on the tide towards the Imperialist Squadron. The Imperialists, with the memories of Kuwagasaki fresh in their memories commenced firing on her, and it was some time before they discovered that they had been wasting their powder on a deserted vessel.

There remained now only the *Kwaiten* and the *Banryu*. In a general attack on Hakodate made on June 20th, these two vessels performed prodigies of valour against tremendous odds. A shot from the *Banryu* fired the powder-magazine of the *Choyo* and destroyed her, and her crew fought valiantly until she at last received her *coup de grace* in a shell from the *Kasuga* which smashed her engines and disabled her. The *Banryu* was now sunk by her own crew, and the *Kwaiten*, seeing further resistance to be hopeless, followed her example.

Thus, was quenched the last spark of resistance to the Imperial forces in Japan. Enomoto surrendered on the 27th of June and the pacification of the country was complete. It is true that we shall again find rebels in arms against the constituted authorities, but Saigo's rebellion was a different thing altogether. He was not fighting, as was Enomoto, for the maintenance of a political system which had been established for many years.

We can feel and admire the loyalty which prompted these men to hold fast to the *Shogunate* from which their families had in the past, received so many proofs of kindness and consideration. This feeling was shared by the Imperialist party itself and the generosity with which the Emperor treated the faithful adherents of the lost cause has done much to heal the wounds of the civil strife.

And what are we to say of Togo's share in these events?

We see in him the patient painstaking officer, diligent in the performance of his duty, absolutely devoid of all thoughts of self, and happy in the triumph of his Master's cause.

We can say no more than that. His ship, the *Kasuga*, did good service in the pursuit of the *Takao*, and the attack on the *Banryu*. His own personal interest in the fight is shown by his involuntary exclamation ("the coward") when he saw the *Teibo* retreating from her position to avoid the explosion of the *Choyo* during the battle at Hakodate. He was for a long time chaffed by his messmates for having "scolded a man-of-war".

There are no picturesque incidents in this part of Togo's life: nothing to strike the imagination of the reader, such as we find in the *Life of Nelson*. His was the life of the quiet conscientious officer, a life not without its effect on those amongst whom it was lived, Togo had already attracted the attention of his superiors and this is proved by his being presently selected as a promising officer, whom it would be well to send to England for further training.

NAVAL BATTLE OF HAKODATE

CHAPTER 5

Togo in England

When the Hakodate fleet under Enomoto had been destroyed the Loyalist troops returned in triumph to Yokohama, and what had now become the capital city of Tokyo, and it was at Yokohama that the *Kasuga* was paid off.

Togo's employment was now for a while at an end. The Satsuma Navy had ceased to exist with the restoration of the Imperial Power, which brought all military and naval forces under the control of the newly-formed central government, and the Imperial Navy had not yet been founded.

Still his heart remained in the naval profession, and the experiences of the Hakodate campaign having been quite long enough to let him know the imperfections of Japanese seamanship, his own included, he made application through the leading men of his clan to be sent to England for purposes of study. He had many rivals to fear, for there was then a desire in every young *samurai* to visit foreign countries and learn something that might be of use to his country and himself, and the responsible officers were over-run with applicants wishing to be sent abroad. His first applications were unsuccessful, but when his fellow-clansman Okubo, was Minister for Home Affairs, Togo made application once more, and after some delay found that he had been chosen.

We can well imagine the anxiety with which he awaited the verdict of the authorities. The Japanese say that one evening a band of Satsuma young men and others, whom the generosity of their ex-lords was keeping in Tokyo as students, unable any longer to restrain their eager curiosity, went to a fortune-teller to learn their future destiny. The fortune-teller, anxious to please, prophesied smooth things, and told the first three or four that they were going to be greatly distinguished, so that everything went off pleasantly until No. 5, a student named Matsuyama, presented himself, much the worse for liquor. Matsuyama was not pleased with the fortune he received, and a noisy altercation ensued during which the others, who had not yet been examined, picked up the fees they had already paid, and walked out in disgust. Thus, Togo was prevented from hearing about his future victories in the seas around Japan.

However, the permission came at last, and Togo, who had been utilising the precious moments in learning English at Yokohama, from missionaries and from the soldiers belonging to the Legation guard, received his marching orders in March 1871.

He and his companions must have presented a strange appearance as they left Yokohama for Europe. There were no tailors, then, for Japanese who wished to be dressed as foreigners, and the future Nelson of Japan started in a second-hand costume which must effectually have obliterated all signs of a destined greatness. He must during his voyage have been continually treated with a good-natured contempt due entirely to his clothes, and yet surely no one ever deserved less to be treated with disdain than did he.

Togo was a fine specimen of the Bushido in which he had been trained. We have seen already, in our account of the *Gochu* or Associations of young men in Satsuma, how the youthful *samurai* of that province were taught to endure pain and to look fear in the face without flinching. But he learned other virtues as well. The short sword in his girdle was a perpetual reminder to him that death was at all times preferable to dishonour, that the remedy for disgrace was in his own hands.

The proverb *bushi ni nigon nashi*, ("the *bushi* has no second word") reminded him of the cardinal virtue of truthfulness, consistency, faithfulness to promise. Fair play and loyalty were ingrained in the *bushi's* character, and the civil war which had just come to an end was an admirable specimen of those chivalrous qualities in action. Each side had treated the upholders of the other side with the utmost respect and consideration. The Satsuma retainer, loyally supporting his feudal lord, was quite ready to accord all honour to the Tokugawa *samurai*, who was only doing his duty by his lawful master. Both parties were united in their reverence for the sovereign, and their only thought was how to deliver him from the mistaken council of the men that formed his entourage.

The sovereign, on his part, recognised the good feelings that animated both parties of his subjects, and when the fortune of war decided that the victory should belong to the Satsuma men, the vanquished were treated with the utmost generosity. The living were pardoned, and admitted to the Imperial presence and councils, the dead were honoured with those posthumous rewards of rank and position which mean so much in the Japanese world: even Saigo, who died in arms against his sovereign, was pardoned posthumously, and restored to his former dignities.

The one exception of this universal clemency has been the unfortunate Ii Kamon no Kami, the Shogunal Prime Minister, and he, undeservedly as I believe, lies under the reproach of not having "played the game" in his dealings with his Imperial Master.

Togo's chivalrous spirit was to be shown years after in the first attack upon Fort Arthur. Ancient etiquette required that the knight should notify his own name and titles to his enemy before commencing a combat with him, and it was absolutely the correct thing for Togo to do when, a few hours before his attack, he sent a wireless message to Admiral Makaroff, advising him to surrender.

How Togo must have rejoiced when he got to know, as he must have done during his time in England, a few of the old-time English gentlemen whose ideals of life and honour were perhaps the nearest approach in modern times to the spirit of the Japanese *bushi*. In the year 1871, Thackeray had not been very long dead—not more than ten years or so:—Col. Newcome and Major Pendennis were types still recognised as being in existence, and Kinglake's "Crimea", with its justification of a noble though much-abused English *samurai*, was still making its vigorous appeal to the English sense of justice. Togo must have been just ripe to appreciate the good side of English life and character.

In London, he met several of his compatriots, Satsuma and Choshu clansmen, such as Kawase, Kawakita, and others who were studying like himself. Kikuchi Dairoku, now a baron, and for some time a Minister of Education, was then either in London, or in Cambridge, and a few others from other parts of Japan were there to form a body round which all the Japanese students in England might from time to time rally.

Togo did not want for companions in London, but circumstances eventually led him to Plymouth, to the training-ship *Worcester*, which seemed to offer him the greatest facilities for obtaining a practical mastery of the details of his profession. The reports sent home about him were so good that in 1872 the government decided to grant him the rank and treatment of a and lieutenant in the Imperial Navy, which had been reconstructed since his departure for England, and when his course of training on board the *Worcester* was finished, in 1876, he was ordered to remain in England to watch the construction of the new Japanese ship *Hiyei*, which was finished in January 1878, and reached Japan in the following May.

The *Strand* magazine for April 1905 contains an article on Admiral Togo "as a youth" in England, written by the Rev. A.S. Capel M.A. to whose care Togo was for some time committed. The writer of this book knew Mr. Capel very well by sight in Cambridge and must have been in residence as an undergraduate of Peterhouse just about the same time, though he never saw Togo, nor even heard of his existence.

Mr. Capel tells us that Togo was put under his care for a few months in Cambridge during the interval between his arrival in England and his joining the *Worcester* training ship.

He knew very little English, and his prepress, partly from illness, and partly perhaps from a natural incapacity for mere language study, was very slow. In mathematics, however, he made much prepress, and soon learned enough English to discuss the problems of that science.

Mr. Capel next speaks of his excellent manners, and tells us how it became his practice to recommend to his other pupils the study of Eastern manners as being so much better than the Western manners which Togo and his brother-Japanese had come to England to team.

His natural modesty is shown indirectly. When Togo was a student in Mr. Capel's house he was already the hero of two or three naval fights, and what would have delighted the children of the house more than an account of the stirring incidents of the bombardment of Kagoshima? Yet, fond though he was of gossiping with children, he seems to have resisted all temptation to boasting, and Mr. Capel writes as though he did not know that Togo had already gone through a couple of campaigns.

Togo's kindness to animals and fondness for children are early traits which are still to be found in the grown man, only with more scope for their exercise, and we are also told of the wonderful power of enduring physical pain which he showed under the operations made necessary by a long and troublesome affection of his eye. It was this affection which caused Mr. Capel to have the lad removed from Cambridge to Portsmouth, and thence to Plymouth where he joined the *Worcester* for special nautical training, and yet from the very beginning he had stated his intention of becoming a "sailor on dry land", by which he was supposed to mean a shore appointment at the Japanese Admiralty.

Mr. Capel incidentally also mentions the young man's fondness for attending church, the singing of the psalms and hymns having a fascination for him, and the use of the English Prayer-book enabling him to follow with a certain amount of intelligence the worship that was going on. I remember to have read some months ago in a New York paper (I am almost sure that it was the *Freeman's Journal*) a statement that the admiral had, during his stay in England, been baptised a Roman Catholic. I have never been able to verify the statement, and I do not think that it is true.

The editor of that sheet published this statement when the "yellow peril" folly was at its height and it was evidently a great comfort to him to think that, if the navies of Christian Russia were doomed to fall before the pagan Japanese, at least the hand that directed the blow was that of a Catholic Christian. It was not much of a comfort, and the little there was in it rested, I fear, on no solid basis of fact. And yet no one can have read the dispatches in which he announced his victories to his Sovereign without being impressed with their deeply religious tone. All wise men, says Lord Beaconsfield, in one of his novels, are religious: all wise men belong to the same religion, but they never say what their religion is.

Whilst Togo was thus laying the foundation of his future greatness in England, great events were happening in Japan. The elder Saigo, the *beau-ideal* of a Japanese *samurai*, and the darling of the Satsuma clan, had put himself at the head of a rebellion, which, though nominally directed against the counsellors who surrounded the sovereign, and not against the sovereign himself, would nevertheless, had it been successful, have ended in the undoing of the whole work of the restoration.

It was due mainly to the Satsuma men that the emperor had got back to his own. They, with their colleagues of Choshu, Hizen, and Tosa, had overthrown the *Shogunate* and restored the personal rule of the sovereign, The statesmen who directed that movement saw that the personal rule of the sovereign was incompatible with the existence of the quasi-independent princedoms which, during the Feudal times, had covered the whole land. Japan, they insisted, must be unified, and in order that the unification might be accomplished, the minor principalities must go, and a strong central government be established. The great barons, to their endless honour, consented to be 'mediatised' and to become the nobility of an united Empire instead of the ruling princes of a divided land.

But further measures were necessary. If Japan was to become a great nation in the modern sense of the term, it was necessary that she should have a strong army, resting not on the loyalty of the military clans but on the patriotic service of the whole people, and it was also of the utmost importance that she should have a period of peace during which to effect the necessary changes.

It was proposed therefore to abolish the special privileges of the *samurai* class by adopting universal conscription, and to take conciliatory measures in the matter of certain difficulties which had occurred in Korea.

We, looking back, with the experience of forty years behind us, now know how wise these measures were. Conscription has made *samurai* of the whole nation, and the present year has seen the sons of farmers and merchants rivalling the deeds of the ancient *bushi*. The breathing space that Japan needed for her reconstruction has been used to the full, and no fear of foreign aggression disturbs the nation.

But in 1875 or 1876 these results were not so evident. Men of a less penetrating gaze only saw that the *samurai* class, the backbone of the nation's military power, was being threatened with extinction, at the very moment, too, when foreign Powers were knocking more loudly than ever at the gates of Japan. It was not unnatural that the Japanese *samurai*, especially those of Satsuma, whose merits had been so great in the troubles which Japan had just passed through, should lift a cry of alarm. Neither was it altogether strange that the rumour of a plot against Saigo's life should send the military students of Kagoshima to arms and at last force Saigo himself to put himself at their head.

It was a most regrettable occurrence, but a natural one, and one which the Japanese have done well to condone. Certainly, no act could have demonstrated more clearly the magnanimous generosity of the Ruler than that which restored Saigo posthumously to his former honours and allowed his monument to speak to his fellow-countrymen of a life which, if at times a mistaken one, was always noble.

Had Togo been in Japan, he would in all probability have 'gone out' with Saigo. Saigo was a Kagoshima man, a former member of the same *gochu* to which Togo afterwards belonged. As an older man, and of leading influence in the councils both of the clan and the nation, he had many opportunities of helping his younger clansmen. His influence had frequently been exercised on behalf of members of the Togo family, and when the Kagoshima men rose and placed Saigo at their head in their rebellion, Togo's three brothers all thought it their duty to support him. The three brothers lost their lives in the rebellion: Lieutenant Togo, living peaceably in England, was saved from the necessity of making a difficult decision, and was thus spared to render invaluable service to his country in the hour of her need.

ADMIRAL TOGO'S FAMILY AND HIS RELATIVES IN THE GARDEN OF THE ADMIRAL'S HOUSE

CHAPTER 6

Quiet Progress

.

Lieutenant Togo returned to Japan on board the *Hiei*, on May 2, 1878, and on the 3rd of July following was promoted to the rank of 2nd lieutenant (*chu*-i). On the 18th of August, he was transferred to the *Fuso*, and on the 18th December received another step, being promoted a full lieutenant (*tai-i*). The rapidity of his promotion may be taken as some indication of the esteem in which he was held by his superiors.

In May 1879, just one year after his return to Japan, he was moved back to the *Hiyei*, and in December of the same year received the rank of lieutenant-commander. In 1880 (January) he went to the *Jingei* as vice-captain, and received the junior 6th grade of Court rank, and in December 1881 became vice-captain of the *Amagi*.

Whilst on board the *Amagi*, he had occasion to see a little service in Korea. On July 25, 1882, he was at Bakwan (Shimonoseki) with his ship when a disturbance broke out at Seoul which summoned him to Korea. A disturbance had broken out in the Korean Capital, and a mob invading the Royal Palace had threatened the life of the queen. That unfortunate lady (she was murdered some years later) had taken refuge in the Japanese Legation, but the mob had pursued her with violence, and, in the attack on the Legation which ensued, seven Japanese were killed. Mr. (now Baron) Hanabusa, who was at that time minister, at length managed, with some of his subordinates, to escape on board a foreign ship at Chemulpo, which took him to Nagasaki, where he was able to inform his government of what had occurred.

The *Amagi* was at once ordered to Korea, and a landing party, of whom Togo was one, marched up to the capital, and, with the good offices of the foreign powers, succeeded in convincing the Korean King of the wrong he had done in permitting a foreign Legation to be attacked.

The *Amagi* then returned to Bakwan, and Togo, whose services were recognised by a present from the government, remained with her until the 24th of February 1883, when he was ordered to come up to Tokyo on board the *Nisshin*. Arriving at the capital, he found that he had been appointed commander of the *Teibo*, a ship which he did not long retain, as, in May 1884, he was sent back to the *Amagi*, as commander, and ordered to cruise along the Chinese and Korean coasts to observe the operations of the Franco-Chinese war which was then in progress It was recognised that he, especially, was the man to whom such an opportunity would be profitable.

At the conclusion of that war, he returned to Tokyo, when he made a special report in person to His Majesty, and was honoured by a banquet. The significance of this is very clear. The quiet, patient, and yet determined officer was making his way up in the ranks of his service.

From June 1885 to May 1886, he had shore billets, partly at the Shipping Bureau of the Naval Department in Tokyo (*Shusenkyoku*) and partly at the Onohama Dockyard. He was then placed as commander on board the *Yamato*, but transferred in November to the *Asama*, a post which held for some time concurrently with the superintendency of the Yokosuka Arsenal (*Heiki Bu Cho*). In July 1887, he was at Yokosuka as President of the Court Martial which tried the case of the stranding of the Kongo. In 1889 we find him appointed to the *Hiyei*, promoted full captain, and advanced in Court rank. In 1890, he was for a short time Chief of Staff at the Kure Naval Station. In 1891, he was appointed to the *Naniwa*, the armoured cruiser which was destined to bring his name for the first time before the world outside the naval circles of Japan.

In this ship, he cruised around the coasts of China and Korea (1892), visited the Hawaiian archipelago to care for Japanese interests (1893), and cruised off Hokkaido and Vladivostok (1894), In that year he had a break for two months on shore as Director of the Kure Naval Station, but in June he was back again on the *Naniwa*, and in Chinese waters, waiting for his opportunities of service in the imminent war with China.

None but a Japanese, or one of those favoured foreigners who have been privileged to see the Japanese Navy from within for a long course of years, can form an idea of the strenuous character of the period which we have been considering in this chapter.

Togo's life, with its continuous changes, and its rapid succession of duties and responsibilities was no more strenuous than that of any of the hundreds of able and ambitious officers who were at this time engaged in the creation of the Japanese Navy as a first-class fighting force.

The material they had to work with was in truth of the very best, nevertheless, the task was a Herculean one. The authorities had to turn the hardy and daring fisher population of the sea-board of Japan into an effective force of blue-jackets, capable of understanding and handling the complex machinery of a modern battle-ship, and worthy of a place side by side with the jack-tars of Britain, America or Germany. In order to do this, a body of able officers was absolutely needed, and though the *samurai* were ready at hand with traditions of military valour, the *samurai* themselves needed to be shown how much more than mere valour was necessary for the evolution of a naval officer.

The *samurai*, especially in the days of confusion and laxity which preceded the fall of the *Shogunate*, had fallen into lawless ways and needed to feel the force of a strict discipline. Instructors could be procured, but education was not so easy. There was a temptation to political activity in days when young Japan was looking forward with feverish anxiety to the gift of constitutional government, which was to give to every intelligent student a chance of political distinction, and it was rather hard for the *samurai*, whose influence had been so great during the birth-throes of the Restoration, to turn a deaf ear to the allurements of party politics. There was also another danger.

Intercourse with foreign nations had revealed to the Japanese the immense wealth of England and America, and the gospel of materialism had come ill, along with other gospels, to break down the old ideals of mediaeval Japan, It was absolutely necessary to keep the Japanese naval officers free from the materialistic notions of the West, and to make them feel so inspired with the dignity of their noble profession that they should value the comparative poverty which their uniform implied above the more tangible comforts of wealth and ease. There was yet another task.

Satsuma men had been the creators of the navy, and their influence has always been very great in the force. But men of other clans were now chosen to fight side by side with these intrepid and hot-headed men from the South. It wanted an infinity of tact, patience, perseverance and good sense to eradicate the clan feeling from the force, to merge all local interests in the higher interests of the Empire, and to make all, officers and men alike, feel that none of them would be left out in the cold, but that, provided a man were a good officer, it did not much matter where he hailed from. The success which attended these efforts was largely due to the patient, self-denying efforts, of that band of devoted officers whom Togo so well represents, and when we think of the glories of the Japanese Navy in the twentieth century we must not forget the patient labours of the latter part of the nineteenth.

Japan is, (at 1903), and perhaps always will be, a comparatively poor country, and her poverty hindered her naval expansion for years. It costs much money to buy and equip vessels of war, and Japanese Parliaments in the early days were not always eager to vote supplies for a fleet, the utility of which was not then as clear to the man in the street as it is now.

The authorities were consequently obliged to go slowly in the work of organisation. It was doubtless irritating to have to do so, but it was good that it was so. The smaller ships were as much as the inexperienced crews of those early days were competent to manage effectively, and by reason of this very tardiness of development the Japanese Navy was probably saved from many of the disasters which other navies have met with even in days of peace. When Togo was appointed captain of the *Naniwa*, that vessel was one of the finest ships of the Japanese Navy.

Launched at Elswick in 1885 and completed the following year, she is 300 ft in length, with 36 ft of beam, and a draught of 18½ ft. Her displacement is 3700 tons, her indicated horsepower, 7235. Her deck armour is 3 in. for gun positions. She carries 2 ten-inch and 6 six-inch guns, steams 18.72 knots with a coal capacity of 800 tons, and has a complement of 350 men. If we compare these dimensions with those of the monster battleships which now fly the Flag of the Empire, they are as nothing. But in 1893 they meant a great deal.

CHAPTER 7

The War with China

Korea had for a long series of years afforded a bone for contention between China and Japan. The friendly overtures, made by the Imperial Government to Korea in 1868, had been rejected by the government of that country, which inclined strongly towards the stagnant decay of the Celestial Empire, from whose rulers it received constant encouragement, a Japanese man-of-war was even fired upon by the Koreans in the early days of Meiji, and we have already had occasion to refer to the attack made by the anti-reform and antiforeign parties in the Korean Capital on the Japanese Legation at Seoul, and Mr. Hanabusa's narrow escape from imminent peril.

Two years later another peril threatened the peace. The Korean reformers under Kim-Ok-Kyun formed a conspiracy to murder their political rivals of the conservative, or Chinese, party during a banquet, to get possession of the person of the king and, to establish a progressive government. In this attempt, they seem to have confidently, though without official authority, reckoned on Japanese support; for Japan, they thought, would naturally be well disposed towards any attempt at progress or enlightenment; thus, when their plot had been, in part at least, successfully carried out, they appealed to the Japanese Legation Guard to protect the Royal Palace and person.

This brought the Japanese into collision with the Chinese troops, who were called in to aid by the anti-reform party, and, a regular fight ensuing, the Japanese and reformers were driven out of the Royal Palace, the Japanese Legation was again attacked and burnt, and the Legation staff and escort obliged to take refuge at Chemulpo, The Diplomacy of the foreign Powers now intervened to save the situation. Korea apologized to Japan, and agreed to pay an indemnity for the destruction of the Japanese Legation, and both Japan and China promised by the Treaty of Tientsin, in April 1885, to withdraw their troops from Seoul. A second portion of the same treaty provided that if at any future time the interests of one party required, or seemed to require, the presence of its troops in Seoul, the other party should be notified of the fact, and be entitled to send an equal force for the protection of its own interests.

The Treaty of Tientsin worked fairly well for several years. The governments of the three countries were outwardly at peace, and the surface of affairs was smooth; but there was much unofficial intriguing going on, and it was just as impossible for the Korean Reform party not to look to Japan for sympathy as it was for the Conservatives to refrain from covert appeals to Chinese fellow-feeling. The methods resorted to by both parties were reprehensible at times, but we must remember that misgovernment always leads to deeds of violence, and the misgovernment in Korea had been long a bye-word and reproach.

The Korean reformer Kim-Ok-Kyun had been obliged to leave his country after the events of 1884. He spent the years of his exile mostly in Japan, in retirement and semi-concealment; but in March 1894 he was at Shanghai, staying in a boarding-house under an assumed name, and was there assassinated by a Korean named Hung. The Chinese authorities arrested Hung, but, instead of punishing him themselves, sent him along with the body of his victim to Seoul. At Seoul, however, he received no punishment; he was on the contrary loaded with honours by the Korean king, whilst Kim-Ok-Kyun's body was quartered and exposed to view in public places in the city.

Everything looked as though the murder of Kim-Ok-Kyun had been done by the order of the Korean Government with the approbation of China, and the indignation of the Japanese, who looked upon Kim-Ok-Kyun as being under their protection, knew no bounds.

The Conservatives in Korea now felt themselves in a position to take more decided steps of a reactionary nature, and for this purpose allowed the *Tonghaks* in the south of the peninsula a somewhat free hand. The *Tonghaks*, originally a religious organisation, had developed strong political tendencies of an anti-foreign nature. In the spring of 1894, they rose in arms and proclaimed a policy of expulsion which was directed mainly against the Japanese, as being practically the only foreign nationality largely represented in the Peninsula.

The Korean Government, professing not to find itself in a position to quell this insurrection, applied to China for help. On the 7th of June 1894, the Chinese Minister in Tokyo informed the Japanese Government, in accordance with the provisions of the Treaty of Tientsin, that China intended sending troops to Korea "for the sake of helping a tributary state" in the hour of need. Japan refused to recognise the definition of Korea's tributary status, and prepared to provide for her own interests. Negotiations were at once commenced, with a view to providing a smooth way out of the difficulties; the Japanese Government came forward with reasonable propositions, which, if adopted, might have brought prosperity and contentment to the much-distracted Hermit Kingdom, and at the same time made it clear that she would not offer advice without being prepared to back it with something more substantial.

By the end of June, there were in and around Seoul some six or seven thousand Japanese troops whose presence effectively caused a collapse of the *Tonghak* rebellion. The Chinese had a squadron in Korean waters, as had also the Japanese, and a force at Asan; but the force remained stationary and inactive, and its commander contented himself with exhortations to the *Tonghaks* to return to obedience, and pompous proclamations about the solicitude of China for the welfare of a tributary state.

On previous occasions, diplomacy had always found a way out of the oft-recurring difficulties between Japan and her neighbours, and this time also efforts at mediation were not lacking. But Japan was determined not to be trifled with. Korea was a buffer state between herself and a power which her statesmen had long had reason to dread. Korea, well governed, might be a real protection. Korea, governed according to Chinese notions corrupted to suit Korean tastes, could only fall into hostile hands. The hour had come for Japan to secure for good her ascendancy in Korea, by shelving how weak a reed China was to lean upon—diplomatic attempts failed, and Japan sent her ultimatum on July 19th 1894.

On the 23rd of July, Admiral Ito, acting under orders from the General Quarters, left Sasebo with the main portion of his Fleet, the Flying Squadron under Rear-Admiral Tsuboi, consisting of the *Yoshino*, *Akitsushima*, and *Naniwa*, being sent ahead to reconnoitre. These vessels, early on the 25th, fell in with the small Chinese cruiser *Tsi-yuen*, and the gunboat *Kuang-yi*, with which they had a fight, the end of which was that the gun-boat was run ashore in a sinking condition whilst the *Tsi-yuen*, escaped only by pretending to surrender, and making off later whilst the attention of the Japanese was engaged elsewhere. The Japanese had been drawn off in pursuit of the Chinese despatch-boat *Tsao-kiang*, (which was captured without resistance), and the British steamer *Kaosheng*, under charter to the Chinese Government as a transport, which was sunk by the *Naniwa*, for refusing to obey orders.

Togo's action in sinking the *Kaosheng*, was severely criticised the whole world over as a piece of high-handed violence. It is therefore advisable to reproduce here the guarded and moderate statement of the occurrence given by the Japanese Imperial General Staff in their History of the War with China. It will show how correct was Togo's interpretation of his duties under very difficult and trying circumstances, and it is a pleasure to think that, when all the circumstances of the case came to be known, his conduct met with the general approval:—

About 10.30 a.m. the *Naniwa* steamed up to a transport which had been compelled to anchor at Shopaioul Island, and sent Zengoro Hitomi, Lieutenant of Marine, with Nenjitsu Waraya, 3rd class Engineer, to examine her. This officer made enquiries of her captain, Thomas Ryder Galdsworthy, and examined the ship's books and papers, from which be learned that the ship was named the *Kao-sheng*, that she flew the British flag, was owned by the Indo-China Steam Navigation Company, and had been chartered for this trip by the Chinese Government. She had taken on board troops, arms, and ammunition at Taku and was conveying them across to Asan. The lieutenant thereupon ordered the *Kao-sheng* to follow the *Naniwa*, which the captain after some hesitation consented to do. Lieut. Hitomi then returned to his ship.

The *Naniwa* next signalled to the *Kao-sheng* to weigh anchor, but her captain signalled in reply that he wished to confer upon some important matters, and asked for a boat to be sent, whereupon Lieutenant Hitomi again went on board the transport. During the first interview the master of the *Kao-sheng* had admitted to that officer that he was not in a position to disobey the orders of the *Naniwa*, and that he was quite willing to carry out the *Naniwa's* orders, but that the Chinese officers on board refused to allow him to do so. He had then asked them to be allowed to land with his own crew, but the Chinese had threatened that, if he attempted to leave the ship or to carry out the orders of the *Naniwa*, they would kill every European on board.

They had also put soldiers armed to watch over the master and mates, and to prevent the engineers from entering the engine room, and when the boat was on its way the second time from the *Naniwa* they tried to prevent the captain from communicating with it. When Lieutenant Hitomi came on board again, the captain told him that the Chinese officers would not allow him to obey the orders of the *Naniwa*, and that they asked to return to Taku on the ground that they had not received notice before starting of the declaration of war. Lieutenant Hitomi felt that this was a very serious matter, as the ship was full of arms and war-material, and returned to his ship to report it.

It was the hearty desire of the captain of the *Naniwa* to save the *Kao-sheng* and the lives of the Chinese troops on board, and several communications passed to and fro between the ships, but the Chinese soldiery only became more violent in their behaviour to the captain, and at last the *Naniwa* signalled to the *Kao-sheng's* crew to leave her at once. This the Chinese general would not permit, and so they asked the *Naniwa* to send a boat to fetch them away. This request could not be granted, for matters were now very critical, and it was quite uncertain what course the Chinese troops might take it into their heads to adopt, so the captain of the *Naniwa* signalled to the *Kao-sheng's* crew to come in their own boat, a course which the Chinese again refused to allow them to follow.

The captain of the *Naniwa* now recognised that the captain was helpless against the menaces of his Chinese passengers, so he ordered the crew to leave the ship, hoisted a red flag at the masthead, and whistled several times as a sign of imminent danger; whereupon the captain and crew of the *Kao-sheng* jumped overboard one after the other.

The *Naniwa* now launched a torpedo, which missed, but followed it up with a shell, which made a hole in the boiler and raised a great cloud of steam and smoke. At this everyone that could swim jumped overboard to swim to land, while those who could not swim remained on board, firing sometimes at the *Naniwa* and sometimes at the crew who were swimming towards the Japanese ship. This happened at 1.10 p.m., five minutes later the *Kao-sheng* began to sink by the stern, and at 1.46 p.m. it sunk in deep water, 2 nautical miles to the south of Shopaioul Island.

When she had sunk, the *Naniwa's* boats managed to rescue the captain and first mate (both English) and a pilot (a Manila man); but the crew were either drowned or shot by the Chinese troops. Most of the Chinese were drowned, only some 160 or 170 men succeeding in reaching Shopaioul Island, where they were afterwards rescued by the German man-of-war *Iltis*, and taken to Chefoo on August 1. Among their number was a German officer, von Hannecken, who had been for many years in the Chinese Service.

The following account of the sinking of the *Kowshing* (an alternative form of spelling *Kao-sheng*), taken from Prof. Takahashi's *International Law during the China-Japan War* may serve to set before the reader the legal aspect of Togo's action in sinking the ship:—

It was about 6 a.m. on the 25th July 1894, that the first division of the Japanese Squadron saw two Chinese men-of-war near the island of Phung-do (or Round Island) in Korean waters.

At 7.5 the fleets approached each other within 3000 metres and began to open fire. It was thus the curtain rose on the first scene of the grand drama of war in the Far East. The encounter raged fiercely for about an hour and a half. One of the Chinese ships, being severely damaged, went ashore, while the other fled to Chelung Bay, to find her way back to China. While the Japanese fleet was chasing the enemy two other steamers had appeared in the offing. They were now near, and it was soon seen that one of them was the *Tsao-kiang*, the Chinese gunboat, and the other was the *Kowshing* which had left Taku on the 23rd, and just now arrived on the scene to play the most regrettable part in the matter.

At 8.30 a.m., the Japanese fleet saw the *Kowshing* passing on the starboard in the distance. At 9.15, the *Naniwa*, one of the Japanese fleet, drew near the British ship, signalled her to stop and fired two blank cartridges. Next, she ordered her to anchor by the signal L.P. Prize officers were soon sent to her, and it was discovered that she carried nothing but enemy's troops. Thereupon the *Naniwa* ordered the *Kowshing* to follow her, and this the captain of the transport consented to do.

Soon after this the captain again signalled the *Naniwa*, requesting that a boat should be sent. When that request was complied with, the captain stated that although he was personally willing to obey the orders of the *Naniwa*, the Chinese officers on board would not allow him to do so, demanding that he should steer in the direction of Taku whence they had come. He therefore begged permission to take this course. Meanwhile the Chinese soldiers on board the *Kowshing* were clamouring violently and angrily threatening the captain and officers with their rifles. In this way, the Chinese soldiers prevented the *Kowshing* from following the Japanese ship, over-ruling the will of the captain. So, the *Naniwa* signalled the British captain to leave his ship. He replied again by signal, requesting that a boat should be sent, but the answer was that the captain and his officers should proceed at once to the *Naniwa* in their own boats. The captain signalled in reply that he was not allowed to come. By this time, the tumult among the Chinese soldiers had assumed serious dimensions. Under these circumstances, there was no help for it but to hoist the red flag at the foremast of the *Naniwa*, in token that firing was about to commence, while signals were once more made urging the captain to leave the *Kowshing* with all speed.

No less than four hours had been spent in fruitless signals and negotiations, as it was the desire of the Japanese to make the Chinese surrender without bloodshed, and then guide the *Kowshing* to a place of safety. The Chinese however were unable to understand the generosity of the Japanese, and menaced their commander refusing point blank to obey the instructions of the *Naniwa*. There was nothing for it but to sink the *Kowshing*, and so in another moment a shell was fired at her with fatal precision. The ship began at once to settle down, and soon disappeared beneath the waves.

In his official report Togo makes one statement which does not appear in the above-quoted passage from Prof, Takahashi's book.

"It seemed to me," he said "that she (the *Kowshing*) was awaiting the arrival of the Chinese fleet," so that it was indeed "dangerous to hesitate any longer."

Professors Westlake and Holland, both authorities on International Law, at once came forward to defend the action of the *Naniwa*. They grounded their defence on the following considerations:—

1. That the ship, though British owned and flying the British flag, was actually engaged in belligerent operations as a trans-

port in the service of China.

2. That the practice of commencing war without formal declaration is one which has found its way for centuries past into the practice of nations: that China was a belligerent, and the *Kowshing*, as a hired vessel in their service, must take the risks of belligerency.

3. That the Japanese were clearly within their rights in preventing the *Kowshing* with Chinese troops on board from reaching her destination in Korea, that they had done their best to take her uninjured to Japan, and that the refusal of the Chinese commanding officer to allow the captain of the *Kowshing* to obey the orders of the *Naniwa* was a sufficient justification for Captain Togo's action.

It may perhaps be noted here that the Master of the *Kowshing*, Captain Galsworthy, had been trained with Togo on board the *Worcester*.

In dealing with the *Kaosheng*, Togo had his first opportunity of putting into practice the lessons of naval warfare which he had learned in England. *Fortiter in re*, he had allowed no considerationsof mercy to interfere with what he saw to be his plain duty to his country under the trying circumstances. *Suaviter in modo*, he had excited himself, though vainly, to save the survivors from the catastrophe, and many of the foreign sailors on board these ships expressed themselves grateful for the treatment he gave them. The European and Chinese prisoners from the *Kaosheng*, and *Tsao Kiang*, were sent to Nagasaki, where they were well treated, the European prisoners being shortly set at liberty.

But for a time, there was great excitement, especially in England, and Togo was afraid that his government might not be able to support him in face of the storm of hostile criticism. Throughout it all, Togo preserved his outward coolness of demeanour, but in his heart there was much anxiety, he said:—

If, my action should prove fatal to the Imperial Policy, and bring my country into difficulties, I will at once commit *harakiri!*

Such was the resolution which he came to in the stillness of a quiet hour of meditation on the *Naniwa* Bridge. It was fortunate for his country that no such drastic measures were necessary for the preservation of his honour.

ADMIRAL TOGO AND GENERAL NOGI TOGETHER WITH THEIR STAFF OFFICERS
DURING THE SIEGE OF PORT ARTHUR

CHAPTER 8

The War with China, (continued)

Togo continued on the *Naniwa* until the conclusion of the war with China.

In the Battle of the Yalu which broke the naval strength of China, the *Naniwa* was the fourth vessel in Admiral Ito's line, being the last vessel in the van line, and followed at a little distance by the six ships of the main Squadron. The other ships in the van were the *Yoshino*, *Takachiho* and *Akitsushima*, the main Squadron consisted of the *Matsushima, Chiyoda, Itsukushima, Hashidate, Hiyei* and *Fuso*, with the gunboat *Akagi* and the converted liner *Saikyo-maru* in the rear of the Fleet and outside the line of battle. Eight of these were protected cruisers of the newest type, all of high speed, with steel-belt protection, and most of them provided with quick-firing guns.

The Chinese Fleet consisted of the following vessels. On the right, the *Yang-wei, Chao-Yung, Ching-Yuen*; in the centre, the *Lai-Yuen, Chen-Yuen, Ting-Yuen,* and *King-Yuen*; on the left, the *Chi-Yuen, Kwang-Chia,* and *Tsi-Yuen*. Out of the line stood the *Ping-Yuen* and *Kwang-Ping*, four torpedo-boats, and two small gunboats. The Chinese were superior in weight, the *Chen-Yuen* and *Ting-Yuen* being battleships of 7,430 tons each, whilst the largest of the Japanese ships was not more than 4,277 tons; but they had no quick-firing guns and the dishonesty of responsible officials had provided them with very defective ammunition and, in particular, with many shells which would not explode.

It was Ito's plan to lead his vessels round the right wing of the Chinese Fleet, and then, turning back, to pass through the enemy's line and engage their ships one by one. His manoeuvre was absolutely successful. When it was accomplished all that were left in action of the Chinese ships, were the two battle-ships *Chin-Yuen* and *Ting-Yuen*, their armoured portions unscathed but their unarmoured parts riddled with Japanese shot, the *Lai-Yuen* which was on fire, the *Ching-Yuen*, and the *Ping-Yuen*. Of the other boats, the *Kwang-Ping* and the torpedo boats had taken refuge in the mouth of the Yalu, the *King-Yuen* and *Chi-Yuen* had been sunk, the *Tsi-Yuen* was steaming for Port Arthur, and the *Kwang-Chia* had run ashore.

Before sunset the two battleships were still unsubdued, and were answering though slowly to the fire from the Japanese ships. Admiral Ito had no torpedo-boats, and no means of resisting a night attack from the torpedo-boats of the Chinese. His ammunition was also beginning to run low, so that he deemed it to be the wisest course to call off his ships and allow the crippled Chinese Squadron to gain the friendly shelter of Port Arthur.

The *Naniwa* went through the thick of the fight. The Chinese fought with great determination, and though the Japanese lost no vessel, yet four of their ships, the *Matsushima, Hiyei, Akagi* and *Saikyo maru*, were so badly injured that they had to be withdrawn from action. The *Naniwa* immediately preceded the *Matsushima*, and yet, strange to say, she escaped with no injuries to herself, and only one man wounded, as did also the *Chiyoda*, which followed next after the *Matsushima* and had no casualties at all. The Japanese attributed the good fortune of the *Naniwa* to the skill with which her captain manoeuvred her, for she certainly never sought to avoid danger, and her firing on her opponents was accurate and deadly.

The Battle of the Yalu ended the naval resistance of the Chinese, who never again ventured to meet the Japanese Squadrons in open action. Port Arthur fell, and in process of time Weihaiwei also surrendered to the Japanese forces, the capitulation of that fortress involving the surrender of all the undestroyed remnants of the Chinese Navy. In all these operations the *Naniwa* bore its part, and though the operations against the Chinese ships in Weihaiwei were mainly conducted by torpedo-boats, yet the four cruisers *Matsushima* (repaired soon after the Yalu), *Yoshino, Takachiho* and *Naniwa* had a constant service to render in engaging the forts which the Chinese had erected at the entrance to the harbour, as also the Chinese battleships and cruisers, which would from time to time come out under the sheltering fire of the guns on the forts, and seek to create a diversion by engaging the Japanese ships.

Weihaiwei surrendered on February 12th, 1895, and the tragic suicide of its brave defender, Vice-Admiral Ting, followed in a few hours. Togo's prudent and careful management of his vessel had brought the

Naniwa to the close of the naval operations with her fighting capacity unimpaired, and his prudence now met with its reward. Just before, or just after the fall of Weihaiwei he was appointed to the command of the Standing Squadron and sent to the Pescadores and Formosa, to assist in the occupation of those islands.

A brigade of 4500 men left Sasebo on the 15th March, on the 233d, the *Yoshino* and *Naniwa* had made a reconnaissance of the island, and by the 26th the whole archipelago was in Japanese hands. On the 30th an armistice was concluded, which practically ended the operations of the war.

Besides his well-merited promotion as Rear-Admiral, Togo received many marks of his sovereign's gratitude. A grant of 500 *yen per annum* was given him, and the 4th Class Order of Merit with the Lesser Cordon of the Rising Sun; he had also more solid proofs of the esteem in which he was held in his appointment as member of the Admiralty Board, as Chairman of the Board of Naval Works (*Kaigun Gijutsu Kwaigi*), and as a member of the Decorations' and Promotion Committee. It was evident that his country meant to make a full use of his powers.

CHAPTER 9

The Retrocession of the Liautung and the Post Bellum Expansion

The retrocession of the Liautung Peninsula will be in everyone's memory. When Japan, by force of arms, had conquered China by land and sea, the treaty of peace between the two countries provided that the Liautung Peninsula, with its fortress of Port Arthur, should be ceded to Japan as part of the spoils of war.

To this provision Russia objected, and not unnaturally; for it was a death-blow to hopes which many of her statesmen cherished though without yet avowing them. On the plea that the integrity of China must be respected, Russia, aided by France and Germany, protested against the cession of the Peninsula, and Japan, which at that moment possessed no battleships except the two battered vessels she had just taken at Weihaiwei, was not in a position to say them nay.

No friend stood by at that moment to see justice done. America was occupied in the settling of her newly annexed territories and had but slight interests in those remote regions: England, with the best intentions in the world, had her hands tied with the coming war in South Africa, and could do nothing to aid a country whose future importance among the nations was only just beginning to be recognised. Japan was therefore obliged to yield, with a sense of injustice at her heart, which became intensely acute when, as a sequel to the protest, Russia and Germany proceeded to dismember China themselves by the virtual annexation, under a flimsy veil of leases, of the Liautung Peninsula and Kiauchow,

From that moment, it became the ardent desire of every Japanese patriot (and who more patriotic than the officers of the Imperial Navy?) to have revenge for the affront which had been offered to the nation, and to recover Port Arthur for the Flag of the Rising Sun. Japan found herself, by the unjust action of the Powers, deprived of all the fruits of her victory. Had she been allowed to retain the Peninsula, she would have checked Russian advances in Manchuria and saved the world the spectacle of a long and bloody war.

As it was, she had to stand by, a passive spectator, whilst her insidious foe advanced by rapid and regular steps towards the attainment of an ambition which meant her own ruin. More than that, her plans for the regeneration of Korea were entirely frustrated. The world may see in Formosa what Japan can do by way of organising and improving in districts where she has an absolutely free hand. Formosa is a prosperous province of the Empire, and the world hears nothing of Japanese high-handedness or rapacity there. Had she a had free hand she would have done for Korea what she has done for Formosa.

But after the retrocession of the Liautung her hands were tied. The Korean Government, shamelessly corrupt, had no love for her, and thwarted every measure she took. China and Russia, but more especially the latter, were every ready to back up Korea in her resistance to Japan, and more than one of the foreign Powers was willing to stand behind Russia. Japan was left practically powerless in Korea, with not even enough power effectively to control her own turbulent citizens in the Peninsula, and with the whole tide of intrigue, which runs so strongly in Seoul, setting in against her.

Her agents may not always have acted with consummate discretion in these trying circumstances, her irresponsible subjects were often times disagreeably overbearing in their demeanour, and one instance at least, the most regrettable assassination of the Korean queen, gave a sharp point to the sneers of hostile criticism about Japanese methods, but it is good Buddhist doctrine that there is no effect without a cause, and if the murder of the Korean queen is looked upon as the effect, the cause, or at least *one* cause, must be sought in the uncalled for interference of the powers, which robbed Japan not only of the Liautung Peninsula, but of all prestige and effective influence in the affairs of the Hermit Kingdom.

The effect of the intervention of the powers was to determine the Japanese to make their country a first-class naval and military power, capable of holding her own against any of the powers, whose jealousy might stand in the way of her legitimate advancement and progress in the future. Japanese statesmen had long foreseen that a war with Russia must come: they now saw that the hour had come to prepare for that struggle.

Togo's work during the next few years was in preparation for that struggle, and we can now see that during the whole period between the war with China and the war with Russia, he must have the soul of the preparations. And, just because he was the soul, his work lay beneath the surface.

In the years that elapsed between the conclusion of the war with China and the commencement of the Boxer Trouble, the admiral was for the most part on shore, engaged in Admiralty work, re-organising the Naval Academy (of which he was for a short time the President) for the higher training of the best spirits of the navy, and bearing his part in the great developments of the later nineties.

How great the development was may be seen from the Statistics of the navy. At the commencement of the war with China the Japanese Fleet numbered 28 warships and 24 torpedo-boats, with a grand total tonnage of 59,106 tons. At the end of the war, what with captures and purchases, the tonnage had increased to 91,161 tons, but the fleets as then organised contained no single unit of really first-class importance.

When the war with Russia broke out she had 7 battle-ships, all first-class, except the *Chinyen*, with a united tonnage which *by itself* exceeded the gross tonnage of the whole fleet at the end of the war with China, 6 armoured cruisers with a tonnage of over 9000 tons each, 18 protected cruisers, 10 small cruisers, 1 torpedo-vessel, 19 torpedo-boat-destroyers, 58 1st class and 27 2nd class torpedo-boats, besides two powerful armoured cruisers on their way to the country.

All these ships were manned with skilful and well-trained crews, whilst, for the necessary accommodation of this suddenly expanded organisation, naval stations, dockyards, barracks, training-schools, hospitals, and stores had to be accumulated or provided. The men who were engaged in the directing of this immense undertaking spent laborious days of drudgery and patient attention to detail, and if the biographer finds but little to record during these years devoid of incident, he can but point to these immense results, and ask, where was the room for picturesque incidents in the busy life which all this work implies?

One fact, recorded by the native historian, points to the thoroughness with which he did his work of inspection. He insisted that whenever a gun was tested, the trial should be made with real shell, and not with any merely equivalent substitute. It was a costly method of experimenting, but it made for efficiency, and it was efficiency that he was aiming at.

Gazetted vice-admiral in 1898, he was sent to Tientsin on the *Kasagi* to observe the situation of affairs, which was becoming threatening. At Tientsin, he played the part of a quiet observer, vigilant but unobtrusive, and he reaped "the harvest of the quiet eye" which such observers rarely fail to garner. The Boxer outbreak, which took the western powers wholly by' surprise, found him fully prepared. When he saw the outbreak to be unavoidable, he suddenly left his ship and hastened to Tokyo to give warning. Thus, Japan was well prepared for the struggle, and, from the bombardment of the Taku Forts to the rescue of the Legations at Pekin, kept well to the fore of the other powers.

The writer of this memoir well remembers the affectionate interest with which the news from Togo at Tientsin was awaited by the officers then studying at the Naval Academy in Tokyo, who were all eagerly hoping for a chance of service in the event of disturbances in China. He will never forget one afternoon lesson which he gave to a class of Paymaster officers who, but a few minutes before entering the class-room, had heard that Togo had returned and that the tumults in China had begun. The discipline of the school required that the lesson should be given, and it was given. But the results were not great. What interest could a class take in Gerunds and Participles when they knew that in less than 24 hours they might be on their way to Tientsin as part of the relieving force? A small band of paymaster-cadets were all that remained for me to teach during the rest of that term.

At this point I should like to say few words about one of the officers who took part in the Boxer Campaign, and who later met his death in one of the early attempts on Port Arthur. The late Lieut.-Commander Shiraishi was not at the time a student of the Academy, but was serving under Captain Hattori at Tientsin. It was he who succeeded in outstripping the officers of the other nationalities in the combined attack upon the Taku Forts, and who procured for the Japanese Flag the honour of being the first to fly from the captured batteries.

A man of tremendous physical strength and most impetuous temperament, he accidentally killed a sentry, whom he found asleep at his post with a vigorous box on the ears, and for this was courtmartial led and dismissed from the service. In consideration, however, of his distinguished services at Tientsin, he was subsequently pardoned by the emperor, and after the Boxer Troubles were over entered the Academy for higher studies. I knew him as a gentle, thoughtful, man, with a strange melancholy tenderness, which I know now to have been the after-glow of penitence for the impetuosity which had caused the death of a fellow-soldier, as well as of grateful recognition for the clemency which had restored him to his former rank and position; and, when I read of his death before Port Arthur, I knew that he had died the death which above all he would have desired. I am glad to have this opportunity of paying even the slight tribute to the memory of a brave and honourable sailor.

The relief of Pekin was a military operation with which Togo had nothing to do. But in his capacity of quiet observer he saw a great deal of Russian methods, and when he returned to Japan it was to put the navy into as effective a condition as might be for the approaching struggle.

The work which now fell to his lot was the organisation of the new Naval Station at Maizuru, a post which effectually screened him from the public gaze. Hitherto, Japan had possessed three Naval Stations, one at Yokosuka, near the entrance to the Bay of Yokohama, another at Kure, on the Inland Sea, not far from the great garrison-town of Hiroshima, and a third at Sasebo in the Island of Kyushu, a few hours distant from Nagasaki. To these were added the torpedo-station at Omiya near Aomori, intended to serve, for the protection of the Tsugaru Straits, between the main island and Hokkaido, and the port of Takeshiki in Tsushima, an island half-way between the main island of Japan and Korea.

For operations in North China and Manchuria the Naval Station at Sasebo was most conveniently situated, and it is from Sasebo that most of the naval operations of the present war have originated; but it was evident that in the event of a war with Russia a naval port would be required facing the great port of Vladivostok, which ought most certainly to have played a large part in a naval war between the two countries. The port of Maizuru, with a splendid bay capable of holding a large fleet with ease, was selected for this purpose, and Togo was chosen for the duty of preparing this new base of operations.

The war broke out before the railway which is to bring Maizuru into connection with the outer world could be completed, and this fact militated to some extent against the utility of Maizuru during the present war; but it must also be remembered that the very isolation of the new port served to make it a suitable place for carrying out many schemes for which secrecy was absolutely essential. It was difficult for the general run of irresponsible war correspondents to pry into the affairs of a Naval Station which was only accessible by a long journey by jinrikisha.

Togo's sojourn at Maizuru, whilst no less busy than the other portions of his active life, was perhaps the most peaceful period of his whole career.

He was busy in the organisation of the new post, and in what he loved more than anything, the study of naval tactics. His subordinates have told us in Japanese books and magazines of the extreme quietness of his methods. One of them said:—

> The admiral does nothing, so far we can see, but lift his hand in salute twice a day, once when he enters the Port Admiralty in the morning, and once when he leaves it in the afternoon.

The words speak volumes for his powers of organisation. The whole machine moved so smoothly that the hand of its director seemed to be absent And yet it was always there in case of need.

His wife and family, the former a daughter of Viscount Kaieda, who had been married to Togo in her eighteenth year, soon after the completion of his studies in England, were with him for some time in Maizuru, though before the commencement of the present war they had removed to their present residence in Tokyo, where the two sons are studying at the Peers' School and the daughter at the School for Peeresses. The family life seems to have always been of the happiest (a fact which may possibly seem strange to the Western reader when he is told that husband and wife had never seen each other until they met for the marriage ceremony), and the family seem to have exercised great judgment in the selection of a wife for their rising officer.

Madame Togo is spoken of as a capable, frugal, woman, excellent in house-keeping, not above putting her own hand to the work of the household and a wise mother in the education of her children, and the admiral has requited her affection for him by entrusting to her sole judgment all the details of the household life. He himself has, at all times, been utterly indifferent to the petty details of housekeeping or the arrangement and decorations of his rooms, and when artists have come to tempt him with the pictures which, to some Japanese, are objects of so great interest, he has always been contented to refer them to his wife.

A keen sportsman, his greatest joy during the Maizuru days was to slip out on Saturday afternoons in the oldest and shabbiest of clothes and to spend the week's end rest in a tramp over the hills, with his gun and the beloved dogs with whom he has frequently been known to share his last *sushi* or ball of rice.

A great part of his enjoyment on such days has come from his keen love of nature. He has been known to go along a lane in which sparrows were feeding on grains of scattered rice, and to make a detour rather than disturb the birds at their feast: and on one occasion, when a country friend brought him a stuffed deer, he turned round and scolded him for shooting a doe with young; for his keen eye enabled him at a glance to tell that the animal had been with young at the time of death.

In his garden, he is always interested. He will work in it himself, and nothing gives him greater pleasure than the acquisition of a rare or valuable plant.

Temperate and abstemious in his habits, he has never been intoxicated, though he makes it his practice to drink *saké* with his evening meal. Frugal and careful, he never wastes a *sen* on himself, and yet he is both fond of company and generous. More than once, when he has been invited to a feast at a restaurant by his subordinates, he has contrived to slip out unawares and to settle the whole account before his hosts were aware of how he had defeated their good intentions.

Strict himself in the performance of his duties, he has always expected the same strictness from those beneath him. He will never affix his seal to any report which he has not first verified himself, and the truthfulness of his reports to the emperor during the present war has been as conspicuous as their modesty. When the first draft report of the initial attack upon Port Arthur was submitted to him, it ended with the statement that Admiral Makaroff had perished with his ship. He said:—

Strike that sentence out, we know that the ship has gone down, but we did not see Makaroff die. He may possibly have escaped, and I should be covered with shame if I had reported the death of the enemy's admiral when he was alive.

In his reports of his victories he has always striven to keep himself in the background, and to speak ill generous terms of those who have worked with him, and more than once he has apologised to his staff for the words of praise which have come to him from His Majesty, as though by accepting them he were defrauding his officers and men of their due.

The partisan feeling of the Satsuma clansman has been successfully sunk in the higher patriotism of the Imperial Service. Keenly alive to the qualifications of those with whom he has been brought into contact, he has always used great discrimination in the selection of good material, and to be chosen by Togo for any particular work is in itself a commendation.

He is affable and courteous to all, especially those beneath him, and he has been known wilfully to shut his eyes to a breach of discipline committed through ignorance, so as to give the offender an opportunity to do better.

Such is the man as depicted for us by his fellow-countryman. Japan is happy in possessing him. We feel sure that the admiral would wish us to add:—

Yes, but Japan has many more as good.

CHAPTER 10

The Beginning of the War with Russia

We have now reached a point at which Togo's history becomes the history of his country.

To the thoughtless onlooker, who only scanned the surface of things, the idea of Japan venturing single-handed upon a struggle with the gigantic Empire of Russia was preposterous. It seemed that the upstart Empire of the Far East was running upon a certain destruction. The leaders of Japanese thought did not take this view, and the result has shown that they took a juster estimate of the facts of the case.

A writer at the beginning of the war says:—

Those who looked below the surface have discovered, that in the hidden recesses of the Japanese heart there lay a strong virility of character, a strength of will, and clearness of aim, combined with a readiness to sacrifice self to the attainment of great national purposes, which made any future, however great, a possibility, and there have never been wanting prophets who have predicted that Japan would, by leaps and bounds, raise herself to a high place among the nations. To such persons the thought of a conflict between Japan and Russia did not seem to be absurdly impossible."

In the spirit of religious patriotism, the whole nation is as one man the military authorities can count with certainty on the bravery and devotion of the armies on the field of battle, while the central government can lay aside all care as to any disaffection or disloyalty at home. The nation is as a unit, and here the Japanese Government has a great advantage over the Russian.

Japan has within her borders no discontented Poles and Finns, no Nihilists, no Anarchists, no Siberian Exiles. What is more, Japan has never been, like Russia, a menace to surrounding nations. She can devote the whole of her energy and strength to the war in which she is now engaged. (Russo-Japanese War, Kinkodo, Tokyo, No. 1).

Intelligence, efficiency, perfection of administrative detail, sobriety, official honesty, all these points were in Japan's favour, to say nothing of the geographical advantages which accrued to her from proximity to the scene of battle,—and against all these advantage, the mere bulk and numbers of the Russian forces never had a chance of success.

It is true Japan entered the contest single-handed, and also that, in the beginning, she had but little favour from the great powers of the West, which feared lest her success should involve a collapse of the *status quo* which European diplomacy finds it so difficult to maintain at home. But she had two good friends, for whose benevolent neutrality she will never cease to be grateful. The two great Anglo-Saxon Powers (if the American cousins of Great Britain will allow themselves to be called Anglo-Saxons) had learned to recognise the bond of common feeling which links them to the Island Empire which claims to be the Britain of the Far East.

The British occupation of Weihaiwei had marked England's disapproval of the highhanded proceedings of the three powers of Continental Europe in demanding the retrocession of the Liautung Peninsula, the fraternity in arms which resulted from the common expedition for the relief of the Legations in Pekin had cemented the friendship, and the Treaty of Alliance between England and Japan, soon we trust to be renewed under more favourable conditions, had proclaimed to all whom it might concern that England's heart was entirely with Japan.

The sympathy of the United States had been expressed in a less formal manner, but was, perhaps for that very reason, all the more spontaneous. It has constantly shown itself, throughout the whole course of the warlike operations, in works of practical sympathy, and its crowning evidence has been the solicitude exhibited by the Great President of that Great Republic for the restoration of an honourable peace. Japan knew that she had these two Powers standing behind her to see fair play, and fair play was all that she demanded.

Perhaps I may be forgiven for suggesting that there was another thought, felt though not formally expressed, which gave strength to the Japanese nation. An attempt was made at the commencement of the war to exalt it in the eyes of Europe (perhaps "degrade" would be the better term) to the dignity (or Indignity) of a religious war, and men talked freely about "a yellow peril" which was supposed to be threatening the common Christendom of Europe and America.

The men who used that phrase must have done it with a quasi-consciousness that all was not just as it should be with the Christianity of so-called Christendom, that rulers both in Church and State had for a long course of years been turning a deaf ear to the "warning voices" which must have reached them time and again during the last seventy years or more, and that at length a Power higher than man's was making arrangements for the purging of His own Kingdom. Europe has no reason to fear the irruption of a horde of yellow barbarians. The barbarians by all accounts are on the other side of the Ural; still the rise of Japan is indeed a "peril" to obscurantism, superstition, and corruption, and what Europe wants is not a crusade a yellow race but a return to vital religion. Europe, faithful to the teaching of the Jew whom she professes to revere as her Saviour, will have no need to fear a "yellow" peril.

I have ventured to digress on this point because the thought of a higher Power, working for Japan, occurs more than once in Admiral Togo's despatches relative to his naval successes, and because it seems right that Japan in the hour of victory should hear the friendly warning which the attendant whispered to the Roman general in the hour of his triumph "Remember that thou art mortal." God has shown great favour to the land of my adopted home. The favours of heaven always imply corresponding responsibilities.

When the admiral was informed of his appointment as Commander-in-Chief of the United Squadron, he was living at Maizuru alone, his family being in Tokyo for the better education of the children. He immediately proceeded to the capital, where he stayed two or three days for necessary arrangements and started directly for Sasebo to take up his command. He was suffering from a bad cold, and from his old complaint of rheumatism, which he carries about with him as a memento of the blockade of Weihaiwei in the war with China, and his family urged him to stay a little longer to recruit before leaving for his command, but he refused to extend his stay. "I always get well at sea," he said as he bade his family farewell.

A relative visited him on board the flagship (*Mikasa*) in Sasebo, and asked him if he had any message to send home. "Nothing in particular," was his answer; "tell them that I am well and happy, and that they are not to distract me by sending letters." The admiral had absolute confidence in his family, and now he wanted to give the whole of his mind to the discharge of his duty. There is something Roman about this attitude of mind. It reminds one of Regulus and Carthage.

The Japanese ultimatum was communicated to the Russian Foreign Minister at 4. p.m. on February 6., 1904, On the same day the United Squadron left Sasebo, picking up reinforcements of stray ships on the way, and reaching Mokpho in the S W, of Korea on the following day. Mokpho was made the first "flying base" of the Japanese Fleet. Togo had before him a double problem. He had, to use Admiral Bridge's words, "to meet a hostile fleet, and to pass a great army across the sea."

In order to do this, he was under the necessity of imposing inactivity on the Russian Fleet until there had been time enough for the Japanese Army to be placed on the continent in such a position as to threaten Port Arthur which was the base upon which it principally relied. In doing this work it was necessary for him to take the utmost care of his ships, which could not be replaced. He had under his charge the whole Navy of Japan, and new ships could not be purchased during the duration of hostilities. Against him was arrayed a part of the Russian Navy, and reinforcements might at any time give a tremendous superiority to his opponents.

It was hailed as a good omen by the Fleet that, shortly before reaching Mokpho, they made their first capture a Russian merchantman, named the *Russia*; and the seamen shouted to one another with glee, "Russia is taken," "Russia has been captured."

From Mokpho, Togo despatched, on the 7th, a squadron under Rear Admiral Uryu to cover the landing of Japanese troops at Chemulpo, an operation which was successfully accomplished. Admiral Uryu found a couple of Russian vessels of war at Chemulpo, the cruiser *Varyag* and the gunboat *Koreetz*, which were both sunk after a short action, as was also the transport *Sungari*, which was then lying at anchor in the harbour. The news of this engagement was the first to reach Tokyo. It took place on February 9th about noon.

In the meantime, the main squadron had proceeded towards Port Arthur, some 400 miles from the temporary base at Mokpho. Before reaching Port Arthur on the 8th, the destroyers separated from the battleships and cruisers, and prepared for a night-attack on the Russian vessels which they found lying at anchor outside the harbour, under the guns of the great forts, and expecting nothing less than an attack from the enemy. This first attack by the Japanese torpedo-boats on the night of the 8th was not a complete success; for none of the Russian vessels was captured or sunk; but the battleships *Retvisan* and *Cesarevitch* were badly injured, as was also the cruiser *Pallada*, though none of them so badly as to be permanently disabled. They all took part again in engagements against the Japanese.

On the morning of Feb. 9, Togo learned from a neutral steamer the results of the torpedo action, which were greater than he had anticipated, and this news decided him to make a general attack, without delay, on the Russian ships with the whole of his fleet. It was about 9 a.m. that this decision was reached: about 11 a.m. the Russians were sighted coming out of the harbour; there was just time for a hasty lunch in the admiral's cabin, and a toast for Emperor and Country, and about 11.20. a.m. the action began, at a long range of about 8000 yards, between the Japanese ships on one side and the Russian ships and forts on the other.

The action was kept the whole time at this great distance, the long range giving a distinct advantage to the superior markmanship of the Japanese, whilst it kept the precious battleships of Togo's Squadron as much as possible out of the reach of danger. The Japanese losses were inconsiderable, some of the vessels, the *Asahi*, *Yashima*, and *Azuma*, escaped without a scratch: most of the others were hit, but none in any vital part, and none, it is believed, by shells fired from the ships, the only Russian guns really formidable at this range being the ones on the land-forts near the entrance to the harbour. The total number of Japanese casualties was 72.

The Russian losses were more serious. Admiral Alexieff reported to his government that the *Poltava, Diana, Askold,* and *Novik* were damaged below the water-line, that the *Cesarevitch, Pallada,* and Petropaulovsk, were all temporarily *hors de combat,* and that the *Retvisan* had run aground.

The Russian fleet, badly damaged, was forced after about four hours fighting to withdraw into the harbour. Had Togo been willing to expose his ships by engaging the enemy at closer quarters, it is possible that he might, there and then, have destroyed instead of crippling the Russian Fleet; but it was only a possibility, and he could not afford to run any risk of losing his ships. The guns on the land-forts were dangerously powerful, and had his fleet been crippled then, the command of the sea would have passed to the Russians, and the war might have had another issue. He did what was very hard both for himself and his men, he turned back in the hour of apparent triumph, and thereby "entitled himself to the lasting gratitude of his countrymen." The ships were saved for the final conflict with the Baltic Squadron.

Togo's next operation was the attempt to block the entrance to Port Arthur by means of steamers sunk in the channel in such a way as to prevent the egress of the Russian vessels. This operation, oft-times repeated, displayed to the full the astonishing coolness and courage of the officers and men of the Japanese Navy, It was in one of these attempts that the brave Shiraishi, whom we have already mentioned, met his death. It was in another that Hirose, the idol of the navy, lost his life. The memory of the gallant deeds of Japanese seamen in the stirring events of the blocking campaign will long remain with the nation; for, indeed, if is doubtful whether the world has ever seen greater heroism than that displayed on those dark cold nights of February and March: and where all were so brave, it seems almost invidious to single out one or two names for special distinction.

The blocking operations were not a complete success, for the harbour was never permanently closed, and the Russians, especially during the short period when they were commanded by the gallant but unfortunate Makaroff, made frequent sorties and reconnaissances, which showed that, in spite of the sunken ships, they could still come in and out. Other devices had to be resorted to, mines were freely planted all over the sea surrounding the harbour, and the big guns of the battleships kept up a continuous bombardment of the town, which must have done much to shatter the nerves of its brave defenders.

Military and Naval critics have found much to praise in Togo's conduct of this part of the campaign against Port Arthur. They have noticed the skill with which he changed his "flying base," first to Mokpho, then to Chinnampo, and lastly to the island of Hai-Yun-tao in the Elliot group, each move bringing the base nearer to the scene of operations, and diminishing the distance to be traversed by ships in need of a replenishment of coal-bunkers.

Another point that has been favourably noticed is the care which Admiral Togo took of his destroyers. Sir Cyprian Bridge writes:—

For the first seven or eight weeks of the war, and perhaps for a much longer period, the whole Japanese force of destroyers was kept at or near the scene of operations, not one having to be sent to a dockyard for refit, and this though they were constantly steaming and frequently exposed to the enemy's fire.

In the China war Togo, as captain, brought the *Naniwa* safely out of a long campaign, with her efficiency absolutely unimpaired. In the present war, the same care for his materials was seen in the splendid handling of his destroyers during the first days of the war. It is true that dark days were coming for him, which we will speak of in another chapter. For the present let it suffice that we have spoken of those early successes, which meant so much for the morale of the forces under his command.

ADMIRAL TOGO EXPOSING HIMSELF TO THE ENEMY'S DANGEROUS FIRE
ON THE BRIDGE OF THE *MIKASA*

CHAPTER 11

Dark Days

The attempts to block the entrance to the harbour of Port Arthur having, in spite of the heroic bravery of the Japanese, failed to effect their object, the Russians constantly succeeding in finding a way out through the obstructions. The Japanese, on April 11 and 12, sent in the *Koryo Maru* to lay submarine mines around the entrance to the harbour, an operation in which they were imitated, if not actually anticipated, by the Russians who sowed their mines all round the Peninsula with a liberal hand. Many of these Russian mines were planted far away from Russian territorial waters, right in the very highway of neutral commerce, others got loose from their movings and drifted helplessly out to sea, to prey upon the innocent craft of other and friendly nations.

The mines were the direct cause of dark days, both to besieged and besiegers.

On the 12th of April, the gallant Vice-Admiral Makaroff, an officer who had the respect of the whole Japanese Navy as well as of his own, put to sea with a squadron of seven vessels, the *Petropaulovsk* (carrying his flag), *Diana, Asksld, Novik. Pobieda, Poltava* and *Bayan.* The Russians passed in safety over the space that had been sown with Japanese mines the day before: the Japanese sentinel cruisers began to retire, thinking themselves to be outmatched, but the wireless telegraph soon brought help from the main squadron, which was lying some fifteen miles to the east of the sentinel ships, and the Russians, unwilling to risk an engagement with so large a force, turned back to the shelter of the Port.

At a distance of from one and a half to two miles from the entrance to the harbour, the *Petropaulovsk* struck on a mine, which exploded, and a few second later the *Pobieda*, coming into contact with another mine, was severely injured amidships, and was with difficulty brought into the harbour.

To the Russians the loss of the *Petropaulovsk* was irreparable. With her went down the gallant Admiral Makaroff, the good genius of their navy, the painter Verestchagin, who was on board as a guest, and nearly the whole of her complement of officers and men. The Grand Duke Cyril was one of the few survivors.

But the Japanese Fleet was also visited by misfortune. The Vladivostok Squadrons contrived to elude the vigilance of the Japanese vessels, and made distressing raids upon Japanese commerce and transport service. The loss of the *Kinshu Maru*, on the 25th of April, was indeed relieved by the splendid heroism of the troops on board who preferred death to disgrace, and committed suicide rather than fall into the hands of the Russians; and when shortly afterwards (on June 17, 1904) the *Sado Maru, Hitachi Maru* and *Idzumi Maru*, with troops and, munitions of war were sunk by the same cruisers, a wave of sorrow and indignation swept over the country.

But these disasters were as nothing when compared with the losses among the vessels of war.

On May the 12th, Torpedo-boat No. 48 was destroyed by a mine which she was trying to explode. On the 14th, the gunboat *Miyako* met with the same fate from a similar cause. On the 15th, an unfortunate collision between two cruisers, the *Kasuga* and *Yoshino*, caused the entire loss of the latter. The *Yoshino* sank in a few minutes, only ninety of her whole complement being saved. On the same day, the battleship *Hatsuse* struck two mines. The first caused comparatively slight injuries: the second exploded directly under her magazine, and the double explosion was so violent that she sunk in a few minutes, only 300 of her complement of 795 being saved. It was afterwards ascertained that the mine which sunk her had been purposely laid for her by the Russian special service ship *Amur*. The *Hatsuse* was 15 miles from shore, right in the ordinary track of neutral commerce at the time when she was sunk.

When the news came to Tokyo of the loss of these two great ships, one immediately after the other, it caused a great sinking of hearts. There were some wise men who shook their heads and said something about other losses. But the naval authorities held their peace, and the newspapers said nothing. It was several weeks after that we heard from London that the battleship *Yashima* had also been lost, on the same day as the *Hatsuse* and *Yoshino*, and it was not until after the final battle of the Japan Sea that the government at length published the news that such had indeed been the case. It seems marvellous to think that the loss of a large battleship should have been kept dark for so many months.

The *Yashima* struck on a mine almost immediately after the loss of the *Hatsuse*, but the wound not being so immediately serious, an attempt was made to save her. She was taken some sixty miles towards the nearest base before the rush of water made it impossible to save her from sinking, and as the long interval of six hours elapsed between the striking of the mine and the final loss of the ships, there was plenty of time for saving the whole of her crew.

It was decided that, as there had been no loss of life, the public at home should be saved from the discouragement which would have come from a full knowledge of the disasters, and accordingly Admiral Togo's telegram which announced the loss of the *Hatsuse* and *Yoshino* was eloquently silent about the *Yashima*. The battleship *Shikishima* which was cruising near the entrance to the harbour narrowly escaped sharing the fate of her sisters, the *Yashima* and *Hatsuse*. She was saved by the presence of mind of Captain Sakamoto of the *Yashima*. On the 18th of May, the navy sustained another loss in the sinking of the gunboat *Oshima*, by collision with a sister ship, whilst cruising in Liautung Bay to support the operations of the army.

This tremendous series of disasters seems to have had no effect on the iron will of brave "Father" Togo, as his officers delight to call him. Very few words escaped from his lips on the subject and he went quietly and calmly about his duties, thereby affording to his subordinates the best possible example of fortitude under misfortune.

The remaining ships had to do double duty now, and an officer who was afterwards transferred from the sunken *Yashima* to the *Shikishima* has told the writer that for over one hundred days his new vessel never once let drop her anchors. She kept constantly on duty, coaling and provisioning at sea, the crew being kept in constant health and spirits by the exciting nature of the duties in which she was engaged. Hers was no isolated case, all the ships were kept equally active, and the morale of the men was excellent.

Tokyo never knew until long afterwards the magnitude of the disasters, and the object of the admiral was to keep his enemies equally in the dark. It is true that the Russian had declared that they saw the *Yashima* strike a mine and retire, but, for all they knew, she had been taken safely to the base for repairs, and so the enemy remained uncertain. Had the Russians known the straits to which the Japanese Navy was at this time reduced, they would have sent forward reinforcements with more confidence, and have struck a blow which would have saved the Fortress and the Eastern Fleet from a humiliating capitulation and destruction.

It is said (I will not vouch for the truth of the story) that the wily old admiral caused several harmless steamers to be fitted with funnels and imitation upper works which at a distance bore somewhat of a resemblance to the ships which he had lost, and that these dummy vessels, anchored in the distant offing, served to make the Russians believe that the *Yoshino* and other ships were still afloat. I do not vouch for the truth of the story; no one in authority has ever told me that it was so, on the other hand no one has ever denied it, and the story has often been told me by the 'man in the street.'

In the meantime, the Japanese land forces were encircling Port Arthur from the rear, and the Russian ships in the harbour were becoming extremely uncomfortable.

From the middle of June, sorties of ships both from Port Arthur and from Vladivostok were of frequent occurrence. Thus, on June 23, Rear Admiral Vithoft, with six battleships, four large cruisers, and one small one, the *Novik*, and ten torpedo-craft, put out to sea, apparently with the object of escaping from Port Arthur; but was met by Togo with his whole fleet, and after some cannonading and torpedo-work compelled to withdraw into the harbour. The Japanese believed at the time that the *Peresviet* had been sunk, and the *Diana* injured, but the belief was not confirmed. The *Sevastopol*, however, struck on a mine which blew a hole in her starboard side below the water-line, and though she was brought back into harbour, it took six weeks to repair her even partially,

About the same time, and possibly acting in concert with their brethren in Fort Arthur, the Vladivostok Squadron again emerged, passed through the Tsugaru Straits into the Pacific, cruised about the east coast of Japan from July 23 to 29, captured some German and English ships, the *Knight Commander* among the rest, and returned to Vladivostok on July 1st. Their object evidently was to draw a part of Togo's fleet away from Port Arthur, and so to give their imprisoned brethren a chance: but if this was their object it failed signally. Togo never removed a single ship. *Kamimura* went after them, and caught a glimpse of them off the coast of Korea; but they slipped away from him in the night and reached Vladivostok in safety.

On August the 10th, a simultaneous sortie was made from both the Russian bases, which, taken in conjunction with the other sorties which had already been made, seems to show that the object of the Russian ships in Port Arthur was all along to escape to Vladivostok. They seemed to have despaired of gaining any success at that port from the moment that Makaroff went down with the *Petropaulavsk,*

At dawn on the 10th of August, the Port Arthur ships emerged for a last desperate try for Vladivostok. There were six battleships, *Cesarevich, Retvisan, Poltava, Sevastopol, Peresviet,* and *Pobieda,* five cruisers, *Askold, Diana, Palllada, Novik* and *Bayan* and eight destroyers. The Japanese sighted them about 11 a.m., but no notice was taken of the move, as it was the admiral's plan to draw the Russians as far as possible away from the harbour, so that it might be impossible for them to retire under the protection of the big forts.

Soon after emerging, the *Bayan* struck on a mine and was obliged to return to the harbour. At 12.40 the Russians were 30 miles from Port Arthur, and Togo ran up his signal for action, whereupon the enemy changed his formation and advanced in single column line, first the battleships with the *Retvisan* leading, then the cruisers, and lastly the destroyers. At 1 p.m. the Squadrons were within range of one another, and a firing began which lasted for about 2½ hours without any decisive results. At 3. 30 both sides drew off, and there was an hour's interval, at the end of which the Japanese advanced to cut off the Russians from their line of retreat This caused the Russians to open fire, to which the Japanese replied vigorously, and a hot engagement ensued, the Russians fighting desperately with the double object of breaking through the Japanese lines of ships, and at the same time keeping open for themselves a passage for return.

In this part of the engagement, the Russians concentrated the whole of their energies on the *Mikasa* which carried the flag of the Japanese commander-in-chief, and the projectiles fell thick and fast around that vessel. It was remarked of Togo that he and his staff remained in a conspicuous place on the bridge, throughout the cannonade, directing the operations of the whole action, and that, in spite of the dangers to which all were exposed, the admiral came out without a scratch. The *Mikasa* had 4 officers killed, 6 seriously wounded, 4 slightly wounded (among these H.I.H. Lieut.-Commander Prince Fushimi, Junior).

At 5.30 a shot struck, the Russian Flagship *Cesarevitch,* which literally blew to pieces Admiral Vithoft, the Commander-in-Chief Admiral Massevitch was also wounded, indeed every officer on the ship, except one, was either wounded or killed. An attempt was therefore made to take the *Cesarevitch* out of the line and this necessitated the breaking up of the Russian line of battle. Shortly afterwards, the Japanese ceased firing, and the Russians, completely broken scattered in all directions, pursued by the Japanese wherever possible.

Many of the Russian ships succeeded in getting back to harbour—the *Pobieda*, *Pallada*, *Poltava*, *Peresviet*, *Retvisan*, *Sevastopol*, and others: of those that escaped, only one, the *Novik*, made an honest attempt to reach Vladivostok, She was pursued by the *Tsushima* and *Chitose*, and eventually ran ashore and, was wrecked on the coast of Saghalien, near Korsakoff. She had the proud distinction of having been by far the best handled of all the Russian ships.

Of the other ships, the cruiser *Askold*, with the destroyer *Grosovoi*, reached Shanghai, the *Cesarevitch*, with three destroyers, took refuge in the German port of Kiauchau, the *Diana* found safety at Saigon. These vessels were all disarmed by the Chinese, German, or French authorities, and were thus placed out of action for the duration of the campaign. The destroyer *Rieshitelni* was pursued to Chefoo by the *Asashio*, where she was captured and towed out of harbour. She had outstayed her 24 hours in the neutral port, and the Russians had had the insolence to throw overboard the Japanese officer who came to remonstrate.

On the same day on which this noteworthy action was being fought at Port Arthur, the Vladivostok squadron put to sea to cooperate with the Fort Arthur Squadron. Kamimura, with the four armoured cruisers *Izumo, Asuma, Tokiwa*, and *Iwate*, fell in with them on the 14th in the neighbourhood of the island of Tsushima. As usual, the Russians turned back on being discovered, and made for home; but on this occasion, they had gone too far south to pursue these tactics successfully.

It was a case of the "*devil take the hindermost*", and the hindermost in this case being the cruiser *Rurik*, whose speed was not so great as that of her sisters, the *Rossia* and *Gromoboi*, she fell a victim to the Japanese guns, being left to the tender mercies of the *Takachiho* and *Naniwa* which came up at this juncture. The *Rurik* was sunk early the next morning, the majority of the crew being saved by the Japanese; the *Rossia* and *Gromoboi* succeeded in reaching Vladivostok in spite of all Kamimura's efforts. They were badly damaged, no doubt, though the precise amount of injury is not known. It is certain, however, that they took no more part in the operations of the naval campaign.

This ended the first part of the naval war. The ships of the Port Arthur Squadron were either lying crippled in the harbour, waiting to be sunk by the guns from the Japanese batteries, or disarmed and out of the combat in hospitable neutral ports. One of the Vladivostok ships had been sunk, the others were helpless in their harbour. Togo's anxieties were considerably lightened, but his labours were as heavy as ever. He had to maintain an effective blockade of the coast, to prevent supplies of contraband of war from reaching the ports of Vladivostok and Port Arthur. He had also to see that his ships were properly refitted and put in order for the momentous battle which shall be described in our next chapters.

CHAPTER 12

The Russian Armada

The reinforcement of the Russian Fleet sent out from the Baltic, and known as the Baltic Squadron, set out from Libau on October 15, 1904, other detachments, sent out later as they were got ready, joining the main squadron *en route*. It was under the supreme command of Admiral Rhodjestvensky, and consisted of 7 Battleships, 2 Armoured Cruisers, 1; Protected Cruisers, 1 Despatch Vessel, 9 Destroyers, 6 Auxiliary Cruisers, I Repair Ship, 5 Ships of the Volunteer Fleet, 7 Transports, and a Hospital Ship.

It had an extraordinary voyage. Shortly after emerging into the North Sea, a most unfortunate error of judgment caused the ships of the squadron to mistake a peaceful British trawler for a Japanese Destroyer lying in wait for a surprise attack, and, in the confusion which ensued, the British trawler was fired on by the Russians and several innocent lives lost. It required a large amount of tact and forbearance to avoid a war with England, where the public indignation was intense; but the good sense of King Edward saved the world from this additional calamity, and the honour was thus reserved for Japan of annihilation, single-handed, the Russian naval Power.

A Conference was summoned at Paris to discuss the questions arising out of the Dogger-bank affair, and the Russians, after a short stay at Vigo in the north of Spain, pursued their journey unmolested. A portion of the squadron passed through the Mediterranean and Red Sea, whilst the rest took the longer route round the Cape. In the middle of March 1905, the fleet had rendezvous at Madagascar where it enjoyed the somewhat reluctant hospitality of the French authorities and underwent the harassing experience of a mutiny among its crews.

In the meantime. Port Arthur had fallen on January 3rd 1905, and the Russian Pacific Fleet, shut up within its harbour, had ceased to exist. This relieved the anxiety of the Japanese authorities, and Admiral Togo was enabled to devote the whole of his energies to the preparations necessary for the reception of the Russian reinforcements.

The fall of Port Arthur roused the Russian naval authorities to a fresh effort, and another squadron under Admiral Nebogatoff was despatched with all haste. This fleet, which consisted of one 2nd Class Battleship, 3 Battleships of the 3rd Class, 1 First-Class Cruiser, 3 Destroyers, 3 Transports, 1 Tank Vessel, 1 Repair Ship, and 1 Hospital Ship, was at Suda Bay in Crete on March 20th, and about a month later joined the First Baltic Squadron, which had in the meanwhile left the French hospitality of Madagascar to make use of the same hospitality, grudgingly rendered, on the coast of French Indo-China.

The Combined Squadron was a truly imposing force, and had it only contrived to reach the Far East before the fall of the Great Fortress and the destruction of the Russian ships therein, might have changed the whole aspect of the war. "Delays are dangerous", and never has the truth of this proverb been more strikingly illustrated than in the history of the Great Russian Armada.

Japanese Diplomacy was very busy during these months, protesting against the abuse of neutrality by the French, an abuse which arose from the fact that the laws of France are different from those of other countries as to the duties of a neutral nation, and not, we may well believe, from any intentional hostility to Japan; though France, as the ally of Russia, had the same sympathy for one of the combatants that Great Britain had for the other. There was also in the Japanese public mind, a not unnatural feeling of great anxiety, as the hostile fleet drew nearer to the limits of the Empire; but, whatever fears there may have been, they were admirably suppressed, and a casual observer would scarcely have noticed them.

Togo himself gave no sign. A few days after the fall of Port Arthur he came up to Tokyo to make a personal report to his Sovereign, and to consult with the Admiralty about future plans for meeting the enemy, and then he disappeared completely from the public observation, only to emerge as suddenly on the morning of the great battle in the Japan Sea.

His conduct during his visit to the Capital was thoroughly characteristic of the man. He was accompanied on this occasion by Admiral Kamimura. Kamimura had, for a short time during the war, been the recipient of much hostile but undeserved criticism from his fellow countrymen. The extremely difficult task had been assigned to him of watching the harbour of Vladivostok, whilst the rest of the fleet was busy at Port Arthur, The Russians had a squadron in that port, not large, but still more powerful than the handful of ships at Kamimura's disposal, and the Harbour of Vladivostok, with its double entrance and the foggy seas that surround it, has always been a difficult port to blockade effectually.

The Vladivostok ships made one or two successful sorties, generally with insignificant results, but the sinking of several transport-ships, the *Hitachi, Sado*, and *Kinshu*, all within a short period of time, had caused the feeling to get abroad that the admiral had not exercised a sufficient vigilance in the discharge of his duties. Subsequent information brought out the fact that the disaster was owing to causes quite beyond Admiral Kamimura's control, and is subsequent brilliant action of the 12th August, which resulted in the sinking of the *Rurik* and the disabling of the other Vladivostok Cruisers, had completely restored his credit; but, for a time, feeling had been very bitter in the capital, a large portion of the troops on board the *Hitachi* having been Tokyo men.

Togo was apparently determined that his colleague should have a full meed of the popular demonstrations. He could not well escape the drive from the Station to the Admiralty, through the vociferating crowds; but when a band of school boys unharnessed the horses from the carriage that was waiting for him to come out of the department, intending to drag him in triumph to the palace, they found that the great man bad slipped out quietly by a side door, and was walking home through by-streets with his daughter's hand in his.

A few days of triumph, counsel, and the enjoyment of home, and again Togo disappeared from the eye of the world, to make his final preparations, and to wait calmly and patiently for the dilatory advance of the Russians. It speaks volumes for the admirable discipline of the whole Japanese nation, that for four months not a breath of whisper was heard touching the whereabouts of the Japanese Fleet, though there must have been thousands in the secret. The subjoined letter, published in the *Times* of July 2nd 1905, tells us about all that can be known of those long days of anxious but confident waiting. It was written by an officer in command of a first-class torpedo-boat to a friend in London. Even today, (1903), the general public only knows about Togo's hiding-place that it was somewhere south-east of Masampho, north of Sasebo and west of Moji.

Dear O,—A thousand apologies for my lengthy silence. We have been and are still busy, busy preparing a royal reception for the guests from the Baltic.

When we of the Suiraidan (Torpedo-Corps) meet ashore, we discuss and often wonder if after all the Russians will come, or will they fail us. Do they know that we are ready? To north-west lies the harbour of Masampho, to south that of Sasebo, while Moji is on our east, and here we are waiting, waiting and waiting for the enemy. Will he never come?

If you do not hear from me when a meeting has taken place, take this as my farewell. I do not expect to see you again in this life, except perhaps in your dreams. When my boat goes down, I shall go too and a Russian ship with us.

It takes her weight in shells to sink a torpedo-boat—it's marvellous how they, the shells, do not hit.

I have seen, not one, but many torpedo actions, and I know. With six compartments in the boat, we ought to be able to close in within 20 yards of the target before she is sunk. If we hit, we shall go down with the Russians; if we are hit, the Russians shall come with us, for the last man alive will steer the spare torpedo in the water. What is life but a dream of a summer's night? Can one choose more glorious an exit than to die fighting for one's own country and for the emperor who is a ruler and leader to the nation's heart?

Does not many a worthy man end his life's chapter obscure for want of opportunity? Then let us uphold the honour and the duty of being Japanese. By going down with them we shall, in a measure, pay the debt we owe for the slaughter of those poor innocent peasants. They too are fighting for their country, so shall *Bushi* honour *Bushi*. There are more torpedo-boats and torpedo-boat destroyers than the number of ships in the whole fleet of Admiral Rhojdestvensky, and if each of them destroys or disables one of the enemy's vessels, it ought to do.

Father Togo, now grey-haired, walks quietly to and fro on the bridge of the *Mikasa*, and keeps silence, so all will go well. Do you remember the story when he went up to Tokyo, for the first time since the commencement of this war? Some public-school boys were determined to unharness the horses off his carriage, at the instigation of the *Asahi*, I believe, and themselves draw it up to the gate of the Imperial Palace. Well, Father Togo got wind of this, and so he sent his chief-of-staff in the carriage, while he was seen, but not recognised, to be quietly walking towards Nijubashi, with his little daughter's hand in his. Will he play another trick upon the poor unsuspecting Russians when they come?

I bid you again farewell. Work, work, and work, for the coming Japan depends on you young fellows.

I remain your ever humble brother,

T. N.

At last the critical day arrived. Togo had staked all his hopes on the Russians choosing the Straits of Tsushima on their way to Vladivostok, instead of going round into the Pacific and through the narrow straits of Tsugaru between the Main Island and Yezo, or of Soya, between the islands of Yezo and Saghalien, and an adverse fate, working against the Russians, had determined them to make the choice that Togo desired.

Thick fogs had covered the seas for several days, and so near were the Russians, to making a successful run through the Straits and reaching Vladivostok in safety, that had they been but a few hours earlier Togo would have failed to descry them, in spite of the warnings received from the scouting vessels. As it was, the fog cleared providentially for the Japanese, and on the morning of May 27, the Admiralty in Tokyo received the following telegram from the scene of action:—

"Having received the report that the enemy's warships have been sighted, the Combined Fleet will immediately set out to attack and annihilate them. The weather is fine and clear, but the sea is high."

To this the Admiralty replied at once:

We wish the Combined Fleet a grand success.

On May the 30th, another short telegram was received in Tokyo:—

The main force of the First and Second Squadrons of the enemy has been almost annihilated. Please be at ease.

A series of most thrilling events lay between those two telegrams. We will follow, as far as possible, Admiral Togo's own account of what took place.

His detailed official report published on the fourteenth of June, begins as follows:—

By the grace of Heaven and the help of God, our Combined Squadron succeeded in nearly annihilating the Second and

Third Squadrons of the enemy in the battle that took place in the Sea of Japan on the 27th and 28th of May.

★★★★★★

Note:—The Japanese language makes no distinction between the singular and plural of a noun, and I believe it to have been the admiral's intention in this place to use the word "God" in the singular, as denoting that Great Power, indefinable, and indescribable, which every thoughtful man acknowledges. It is the further belief of the Japanese that the Spirits of the dead patriots remain as something more than interested spectators, actively aiding in the promotion of the country's welfare, and that this is especially the case with the Spirits of the Imperial Ancestors who "stand by" with ever-ready assistance in the needs of the beloved land. It will be seen that the admiral recognises this belief in the concluding words of his report. The victory is there stated to be due to the "illustrious virtues of the emperor." His Majesty enjoys "the unseen protection," for himself and his subjects, "of the spirits of our Imperial Ancestors," and these again have power with God, whose grace and help is also to be acknowledged.

★★★★★★

CHAPTER 13

The Fight

(A) THE SITUATION AT THE COMMENCEMENT OF THE BATTLE.

"On the appearance of the enemy's fleet in the South Seas, our fleet, in obedience to orders from the superior authorities, determined upon a plan of attacking the enemy in our own territorial waters, and we therefore concentrated our force in the Korean Straits and quietly awaited the approach of the enemy.

After a temporary sojourn on the coasts of Annam (it was there that the two Russian fleets effected their junction), the enemy slowly approached us from the south, and I consequently posted a cordon of scouting vessels along the southern limits of our sphere for some days previous to the estimated arrival of the enemy in our territorial waters. The various fighting sections of the Fleet, each at its own base, stood prepared for action and ready to emerge at a moment's notice.

At 5 a.m. on the 27th May a wireless telegram from the *Shinano Maru*, scouting in southern waters, announced the appearance of the Russians at a point significantly marked 203 on the Japanese naval charts, and also informed the commander-in-chief that their ships were apparently heading for the Eastern Channel of the Korean Straits. It is almost needless to explain that the island of Tsushima, lying half way between Japan and Korea, divides the Strait into two Channels, and that the Eastern Channel is the one nearer to Japan. The whole Fleet was at once filled with bustle, excitement, and joy,—a joy which was only made the greater when, two hours later, the scouting ship *Izumi* reported that the Russians were 25 miles N.W. of Ukushima, and steering in a N.E. direction.

Between 10 and 11, Vice-Admiral Kataoka's cruisers got into actual touch with, the enemy, between the islands of Iki and Tsushima, as did also the Detachments under Rear-Admiral Togo and Vice Admiral Dewa, and in this way, in spite of the thickness of the fog, the commander-in-chief was kept constantly informed as to both the whereabouts and the strength of the enemy's fleet. A Japanese officer, present at the battle, has spoken in the highest terms of the services rendered in the early part of the battle by the cruisers under Admiral Kataoka's command. They were none of them powerful vessels, but they made a bold dash for the enemy whom they succeeded in deceiving into a belief that only a part of the Japanese Fleet was opposing them, and by this ruse succeeded in luring them on to the trap which the commander-in-chief had laid for them. It is better to give him this title in this and the following chapters, so as to prevent any confusion arising between him and Rear-Admiral Togo, who also took a leading part in the battle.

By means of the intelligence thus received, the commander-in-chief was able to discover all he needed to know about his adversaries. At a council of war, held in Admiral Rohdjestvensky's cabin, it had been decided, apparently by the votes of the younger men against the elder, to "emulate the deeds of Nelson" and seek the Japanese Squadron in the Tsushima Straits where, it was most likely to be. This resolution was arrived at whilst the ships were in the China Sea, sometime after leaving the Sea of Annam. The signal announcing this decision had been received with enthusiasm by the whole fleet. On the 18th of May, the Russian admiral has given another signal: "the destiny of Russia will be decided within a week. Be ready to sacrifice yourselves for the fatherland"; and on the 19th they had passed the Balintang Channel north of Luzon, and were heading due north in the direction of Tsushima.

The commander-in-chief further learned that practically the whole of the Baltic fleet was on its way through the Tsushima Straits, that the Russians were disposed in double-column formation, with their main strength at the head of the column, and their special service ships in the rear (a formation which would have been an absolutely correct one, had Rhodjestvensky been, as he supposed, in the proximity of a small Japanese force only), and that they were steaming in a north-easterly direction at about twelve knots an hour.

From these data he was able to decide that the general engagement would begin about 2.p.m that day, and that it would be his wisest plan to await the enemy with his whole strength near Okinoshima, and make an attempt to smash the head of his left column. About noon, his main fleet had assembled about ten miles north of Okinoshima. It consisted of a battleship squadron under Rear-Admiral Togo, an armoured cruiser squadron under Vice-Admiral Kamimura, a squadron of smaller cruisers under Vice-Admiral Uryu, the hero of the action at Chemulpo, with various flotillas of destroyers, and was joined a little later by Kataoka and Dewa with their ships.

At 1.45, the commander-in-chief first sighted the enemy, a few miles to the south, coming, as his information had led him to expect, in double column, with their main strength at the head. At the head of the right column were four battleships of the *Borodino* type while the vanguard of the left column, consisting of the *Oslabya, Sissoi Veliky, Navarin,* and *Admiral Nakhimoff,* was followed by the *Nicholai* and three coast defence ships. Between the two columns, and guarding the front, were the cruisers *Zemstchug* and *Isumrud,* whilst behind the battleship columns could be seen, extending for many miles through the mist, a long line of ships, a cruiser detachment consisting of the *Aurora, Oleg* and cruisers of the 2nd and 3rd class, the *Dmitri Donskhoi, Vladimir Monomach,* &c. &c.

The commander-in-chief had calculated in the forenoon that he would begin the battle about two o'clock that afternoon. It was actually at 1.55 that he gave the signal which in after years will rank with Nelson's Trafalgar message:

> The rise or fall of the Empire depends upon the result of this engagement: do your utmost, every one of you.

Never was a nobler message given to a fleet on the eve of a momentous battle. At that instant the Fate of Japan actually did tremble in the balance. The slightest mistake, or mischance, at that moment, would have meant the loss of all the advantages which the valour of the Japanese armies had gained on the continent, in Manchuria, and Korea. It would have meant more: the very existence of Japan as an independent nation was at that moment at stake.

It was a moment of breathless excitement as the battleships steamed off in a S.W. direction for a few minutes, and then suddenly veering to the east, made an oblique movement towards the Russian column. In a few moments the Armoured Cruiser Squadron had joined the battleships, whilst the smaller cruisers and ships, under Dewa, Uryu, and Togo, steamed away to the south, and enveloped the doomed battleships in the rear.

(b) The Attack on the Main Squadron.

It was the commander-in-chief's object, as was shown in the previous chapter, to concentrate the main portion of his forces on the eight battleships that led the van of the Baltic Squadron: for, if these were once destroyed or crippled, the rest of the *Armada* would be entirely at his mercy.

His ships, therefore, were directed towards the head of the enemy's line. At 2.08 the enemy opened fire, at a long range. The Japanese made no reply until within 6000 metres, when they concentrated their fire first on the *Oslabya*, the leading ship of the enemy's left column, which was in a very short space of time obliged to retire from the line, with many wounds in vital spots, and fires breaking out in two or three places.

The next ships singled out for the concentrated fire of the Japanese battleships and cruisers, which became more deadly as the distance that separated the Fleets became diminished, were the *Kniaz Souvaroff* and *Imperator Alexander III*, which were likewise obliged to retire from the fighting line. The *Oslabya* sunk at 3.10 p.m., the other two were quite crippled, the *Zemtchug* was also disabled, and the issue of the battle was speedily decided, for the enemy's line was broken, and he was already thinking more of flight than resistance.

The bombardment of the battleships was now continued for about two consecutive hours without any incident of note, the Russians lying helpless in the hands of the Japanese ships which sailed round them as they pleased, inflicting a continuous series of wounds from their heavy guns, to which the Russians were able to make but a poor reply, inasmuch as, in addition to the general inferiority of their marksmanship, they had to contend with rolling waves which distressed them considerably, whilst, owing the superiority of their position, the Japanese did not suffer so much.

The lift in the fog which gave the Japanese a view of the enemy, at the very nick of time, together with the wind and waves, which remained constantly adverse to the Russians, have by many Japanese been considered to be providential features of this battle

One "stirring incident" to which the commander-in-chief gives special prominence, was an attack by destroyers, under Hirose and Suzuki, on the disabled *Kniaz Souvaroff*, which was lying outside the fighting line, but still able to fire her guns from time to time. Hirose's boats do not seem to have effected very much against her, but the Suzuki flotilla made a more successful attack. The battleship was observed to list heavily to the portside, but remained afloat until 7.20, when she was torpedoed by boats of the Fujimoto destroyer flotilla.

The remnants of the Russian battleships now tried to escape southward, pursued by the armoured cruisers of the Japanese. The battleships followed at a more leisurely pace, taking occasional shots at the smaller ships of the Russians, which had been following their battleship line at the commencement of the engagement, and, a thick fog coming on, these two divisions of the Japanese Squadron lost sight of each other for several hours.

During the period of separation the battleships first attacked (about 5. 40. p.m.) and sank the Russian special service ship *Ural*, and then, discovering through the fog a group of six large Russian vessels trying to escape to the north-east, delivered an attack which lasted from 6 p.m. to sunset. In this engagement, a vessel with a heavy list, and supposed to be the *Alexander III*, was observed by the battleships to capsize and sink, while, another vessel, supposed to be the *Borodino*, exploded and sank, within view of the cruiser squadron which we saw go off in pursuit of the Russian fugitive battleships. Evening was now rapidly coming on, and it was impossible, in the dim light, to make out the ships exactly, but certainly these two vessels disappeared beneath the waves about this time.

At 7.38, the commander-in-chief ordered the dispatch-boat *Tatsuta* to convey orders to the fleet to rendezvous at Ullundo for the fight on the morrow.

(C) THE ATTACK ON THE SMALLER CRUISERS.

Whilst the battleships and armoured cruisers were thus engaged in smashing the head of the Russian line, the smaller vessels which brought up their rear were being dealt with by detachments under Rear-Admirals Dewa and Uryu, and Captain Togo Masamichi. (*Two* captains and *two* admirals of the name of Togo were engaged in the Battle of the Japan Sea.)

These divisions received their orders form the commander-in-chief at 2. p.m., five minutes after the signal for the battleships and cruisers had been given, and at once proceeded, in reversed line, with the enemy on the portside, to attack the rear of the Russian fleet, the ships for special service and the cruisers *Oleg, Aurora, Svietlana, Almas, Dmitri, Vladamir Monomach &c.*

The Japanese vessels which had the advantage of superior speed, opened fire at 2.45 p.m. and by constantly changing their course and firing upon the Russians from every-varying directions, soon contrived to disconcert them entirely. Futile efforts were made by *Aurora* at 5. p.m., and by some destroyers at 3.40 p.m., to break through the Japanese lines, but by four o'clock the Russians had been broken, their ships were separated from each other and damaged, and some of the special service ships disabled. At 4.20 two of these vessels, presumably the *Anadyr* and *Irtish*, were sunk by the Uryu detachment: at 4.40 four Russian coast defence vessels and small battleships, joined their distressed cruisers; but the Japanese had also received reinforcements by the arrival of Captain M. Togo's detachment, and thus conditions were about equalised.

A severe engagement ensued, the severity being measurable by the injuries received by the Japanese ships. Dewa's flagship, the *Kasagi*, was obliged to retire from action, and, accompanied by the *Chitose*, to seek the shelter of Aburadani Bay. Her injuries were so severe that she was obliged to withdraw from the action altogether. Rear Admiral Dewa transferred his flag eventually to the *Chitose* and returned to the scene of battle: in the meantime, the command of both detachments had devolved on Admiral Uryu. At 5.10 Uryu's flagship, the *Naniwa*, was obliged to retire, with a hole in the stern below the water-line; but her retirement did not affect the issue.

The armoured cruiser squadron, which had gone off into the fog in pursuit of the Russian battleships, now returned, and by 5.30 p.m. the whole of the Russian Fleet was in flight, and pursued by the Uryu and Togo squadrons. The pursuit went on until 7.20, when the commander-in-chief's signal of recall was received. During the pursuit, the Japanese sunk the special service ship *Kamchatka*, and the *Kniaz Souvaroff*, which, though long disabled, and twice torpedoed, kept firing her stern guns to the last.

(D) THE NIGHT ATTACK BY THE TORPEDO-BOATS AND DESTROYERS.

When Admiral Togo sent a message to his cruisers and battleships, bidding them desist from their pursuit and rendezvous at Ullando, he had no intention of ceasing his action. He was merely changing his weapons of attack.

During the whole of the 27th, a strong southwesterly gale with heavy waves, had made the management of small vessels almost impossible. The admiral had therefore ordered all this torpedo-boats to assemble in the sheltered Bay Miura, and there to await his further orders.

At sunset the wind abated, but the sea was still very high, and the commander-in-chief still hesitated about using his small craft under such unpropitious circumstances. But the zeal of the Japanese officers and men was not to be denied by such trifles as winds and waves. Without any orders, they assembled at their proper stations, ready for action, and their intrepidity made it impossible to deny their wish. It was a race for distinction. Fujimoto's destroyers pressed on the enemy from the north, destroyers and torpedo-boats under Yajima and Kawase came from the north-east, Yoshijima's boats from the east, Hirose's destroyers from the south-east, whilst yet another group under Fukuda, Otaki, Kondo, Aoyama and Kawada, pressed on the ships from the south.

At 8.15 p.m., the torpedo attack commenced, at a close range, and continued until 11 p.m. The official report of the commander-in-chief describes, the engagement as "a terrible *mêlée*." At the end of it the Japanese had lost 3 torpedo-boats sunk, and seven injured, with comparatively heavy casualties, but the Russian losses had been much more severe: the battleship *Sissoi Veliky*, and the armoured cruisers *Admiral Nakhimoff* and *Vladimir Monomach*, were practically wrecked, unable either to fight or to steam. These vessels did not sink at once.

The *Sissoi Veliky* floated about all night, and her crew were taken off by the Japanese before she went down, about eleven the next morning. The crews of the two cruisers which sunk about 10 a.m. were likewise saved by the Japanese. It was impossible, however, for the Japanese to rescue the crew of the *Navarin*, which was torpedoed about 2. a.m. by the destroyers under Commander K. Suzuki. This ended the night attack.

The waves, which, it had been feared, would be prejudicial to the action of the torpedo-boats were providentially favourable to the Japanese. The tossing of the vessels distracted the Russian aim, and the small craft were thus able to creep up within a very short distance of their enemy, who were constantly exposed below the water-line owing to the motion of the waves.

(E) THE SECOND DAY OF THE BATTLE.

The commander-in-chief was already secure of his victory, but something more than a simple victory was required to assure the safety of his country. It was essential that the Russian fleet should be so completely annihilated that further operations by sea should become absolutely needless, and that nothing more than an insignificant remnant should escape to bring the news to Vladivostok.

In his desire to accomplish this great object he had, during this battle, departed from his usual cautious custom of never exposing his ships to danger. It is true that Fortune had favoured him, and that none of his important units had been lost; but every single ship had been at times exposed to great danger from hostile shots, and more than one of them bore signs of combat on their hulls and upper works. It was this desire, too, which had induced him, in spite of the roughness of the waves, to allow his eager torpedo-craft to go forth, and continue during the night the work which his battleships and cruisers had so excellently done through the day.

The torpedo-craft were still busy with their task when the day dawned; and the battleships and cruisers began to make ready for new ventures. During the whole of the 27th the fog had been intermittent, so that the enemy were sometimes hidden and sometimes visible: the night also had been foggy, and the broken remnants of the Russian fleet had some apparent hopes of escaping safely under the cover of the friendly mist. But once more the "stars in their courses" fought against the Russian, as they did against Sisera of old: the day broke clear and fogless, and the tell-tale streaks of black smoke on the horizon revealed the whereabouts of the fugitive Russians.

Chase was at once given by battleships and cruisers alike, and by 10.30 a.m. the runaway squadron had been overtaken. These vessels proved to be the battleships *Nicolas I.* and *Orel*, the coast defence vessels. *General Admiral Apraxine* and *Admiral Seniavin*, together with the cruiser *Izumrud* which had at the beginning been at the head of Russian line of battle. One of these vessels, the *Isumrud*, made good her escape. She was found some time afterwards on the coast of the Maritime Province, not far from Vladimir Bay, where she had evidently been run ashore by her crew, who escaped with everything on board that was worth removing, leaving her battered hull alone as a lasting monument to the efficiency of Japanese artillery. The other four vessels under Rear-Admiral Nebogatoff were too much injured either to escape or to continue the tight, and surrendered to the Japanese almost without a contest.

Whilst this was going on, the *Otowa* and *Niitaka* attacked the Russian cruiser, *Svietlana*, and sunk her off Chuk-pyon Bay at 11.06 a.m. The destroyer *Bystri* which accompanied the *Svietlana*, was attacked by the *Niitaka*, (afterwards joined by the destroyer *Murakumo*), and destroyed some 5 miles further north, at 11.50 a.m., the survivors in both these cases being taken off by the commissioned cruisers *America* and *Kasuga*.

About 3 p.m., the *Iwate* and *Yakumo* overtook the *Admiral Ousha-koff*, which they sunk after a short engagement. A little later, the *Sasanami* and *Kagero*, destroyers, captured the Russian destroyer *Biedovi*, a capture of some importance, as the Russian commander-in-chief lay wounded on her; whilst the *Iwate* and *Yakumo*, accompanied by the destroyers *Asagiri*, *Shirakumo* and *Fubuki*, made an attack on the *Dmitri Domkoi*, which was discovered the next morning sunk in shallow water off the eastern shore of Ullondo Island, her crew having escaped safely to shore where they were taken by the Japanese.

Other captures were the *Sissoi Veliky*, *Admiral Nakhimoff* and *Vladimir Monomach*, already mentioned. All three ships sank shortly after their surrender, as did also the *Gromki* destroyer, which went down at 12.43 p.m., her crew safe in Japanese hands.

Thus ended the great Battle of the Japan Sea. Of the 38 vessels with which the Russian Armada had essayed the passage of those narrow water, only one cruiser, the *Almaz*, and one destroyer, the *Bravi*, reached the port of Vladivostok, Of the rest some were captured, and more were sunk, some escaped to Manila or Shanghai, where they were disarmed, one was missing,—three or four weeks later a solitary Russian transport, with wounded soldiers on board, made its sad way into the harbour of Diego Suarez on the coast of Madagascar.

Japan breathed again, and well she might. For the second time in her history she had been delivered from the danger of a great hostile *Armada*.

The Japanese, who stood ready to lose their all on the issue of the day, had lost a few small torpedo-boats, and their casualties amounted to 113 killed and 424 wounded.—a total casualty list of 537. Some of their ships had been knocked about by Russian shells, but others, such as the *Itsukushima*, and *Chinyen*, and a few torpedo boats and destroyers had absolutely no losses to record. On the other hand, of the estimated force of 18000 men on board the Russian Squadrons, 14000 had gone down with their ships, 3000 had been made prisoners, and only 1000 men, more or less, had succeeded in malting their escape.

The great victory, which will live forever in the history of Japan and the civilized world, is ascribed to the virtues of the Great Emperor, whose wise and enlightened rule has made possible the rise of his country, to the loyal work of many years of naval expansion, to the wisdom and prudence of the commander-in-chief, to the valour and discipline of the officers and men under his command,—and, when all that has been said, above all, to the invisible aid of those heavenly powers whom every Japanese acknowledges in his inmost heart

It is premature as yet to institute comparisons between Togo, who is yet alive, (1903), who all manner of possibilities before him of future glories, and any great hero of the past, whose record of actions is all made up. We will wish him a long life of distinguished usefulness; and when at length it is closed, and the whole tale of service is completed, no Englishman will grudge him his proper place amongst the great seamen of the world,—even though that place should involve the dethroning of our own great Nelson.

We conclude this chapter with a striking leader from the London *Times* published soon after the receipt of the telegraphic news announcing the victory:—

The further details of Togo's great victory that continue to arrive cannot add anything to the impressiveness of the result, to which they add confirmation which was hardly necessary. 'The Russian Fleet is practically annihilated,' was the first message of the great admiral, and all that subsequent information can do is to eliminate the qualifying adverb. It was the aim of the Japanese not merely to defeat the Russian fleet, but to destroy it, and what they determined to do they have done, as Togo's battle signal bade them do, to "their utmost." It may be a long time before we learn authoritatively and fully how the thing was done, but the stupendous feat for the present holds the imagination so powerfully as almost to stifle curiosity.

There is, however, one thing upon which this is the time to insist, with the great fact standing alone before the world. Whatever the methods, whatever the means employed, we have to account for the collision of two great fleets, so equal in material strength that the issue was thought doubtful by many careful statisticians, ending in the total destruction of one of them and in the immunity of the other from damage greater than might well be incurred in a mere skirmish. The fishing boats on the Dogger Bank were hardly more helpless before the Russian guns than the Russian fleet has proved in the hands of Admiral Togo.

The final explanation is not in ships or in guns or in seamanship or in tactics. It is to be sought in moral character, in lofty ideals, in resistless enthusiasm, and in a universally diffused sense of duty and of patriotism. Without complete confidence in the moral qualities of those to whom Togo addressed a final message almost identical with that of our own Nelson, he could never have dared to divide his forces in order to surround the Russian fleet. Without the most complete response on the part of those under his command, the attempt must have led to disaster. With anything like parity of moral qualities among his adversaries he could not have ventured upon tactics so ambitious and so daring.

But he measured, as the Japanese commanders on land have always measured, the moral and intellectual gifts of his opponents no less than their material resources. The man who sees can judge the errors of the blind, but the blind have no means of estimating the capacity of him who sees. The possessor of high moral qualities can measure the results of their absence in his adversary, but the adversary has no due to the operation of qualities he does not own.

The Tsushima victory is the outcome of *Bushido*, of the training of the Japanese people in the great fundamental principles of human conduct. That training is not a veneer which can be put on for a given purpose. It is a thing which must begin with the cradle and which must be universal in a nation which hopes to come through the last ordeal as the Japanese have done. Which thing may well give this nation pause, and set It considering whether there are not greater ideals than buying in the cheapest market and obtaining the greatest average return upon capital.

ADMIRAL TOGO VISITING VICE-ADMIRAL ROHDJESTVENSKY AT
THE NAVAL HOSPITAL AT SASEBOHOSPITAL

CHAPTER 14

An Expert's Criticisms

It is not for me, a landsman, to attempt to criticize the strategy of the great battle. I am fortunately spared the necessity of having to do so by the fact that other and better men have already spoken, so that I need but reproduce their words with the assurance that by so doing I am giving my readers better matter than any that comes from my own pen. There is no greater authority on all things naval than Captain Mahan and his recent articles in *Collier's Magazine*, though based on telegraphic information only, seems to sum up the situation accurately, I give them *in extensor:*—

At the beginning of any inquiry into the lesson derivable from the Battle of the Sea of Japan, we are met, I fear, by the condition which must be plainly enunciated, at whatever expense to national susceptibility, that there has been no approach to equality in the efficiency of the opposing ships' companies. For this inferiority on the part of the Russians there may be good reasons, which will transpire later; but the fact remains, and it cannot but modify and colour all deductions which may be made.

For one thing, it must, in my opinion, force our attention to fasten chiefly upon the proceedings of the Japanese admiral. His own personal skill and sound judgment, now attested and matured through a year's experience of active war, under varying conditions, make it probable that in the outlines of his conduct we see manifested the convictions reached by a naval officer who, beyond the others at the present moment, can appreciate with the accuracy of intimate acquaintance what are the real possibilities open to each branch of naval warfare. His convictions rest, too, upon knowledge of the results attained, and attainable, in the use of their weapons by the officers and men under his own command, the high training and efficiency of whom have compelled universal admiration.

Hence, the course pursued in this great naval battle has been grounded upon no *a priori* reasoning alone. It has rested upon a large acquired knowledge of the powers of the torpedo and the gun, of the battleship and the torpedo vessel, obtained under severe conditions of war and weather, which usually are largely corrective, not merely of bare theory, but even of the instructive actual practice carried on in peace and in summer manoeuvres.

To the chastened and quickened knowledge thus derived, which invests with unique authority the procedures of Togo, must be added the fact the Russian admiral abandoned to him the initiative, thus permitting him freely to adopt the course which to him seemed best to suit the capacities of his ships. The superior speed of the Japanese vessels would probably in any event have ensured this advantage; the fastest fleet has the weather gauge; and Togo doubtless counted on it from the first. His action, therefore, may be fairly assumed to reflect his ripened convictions, in themselves no mean contribution to the determination of naval problems.

I wonder if I may be pardoned a very short historical digression, entirely pertinent to Togo's course, in noting that the Press dispatches give us as his preliminary step a signal entirely parallel almost identical, with that of Nelson at Trafalgar:

The destiny of our empire depends upon this action. You are all expected to do your utmost.

I should scarcely have noted this resemblance, obvious though it is, had not a prominent Japanese official committed himself to the expression that to the Japanese temper such a reminder was not needed; each Japanese so expected of himself. Doubtless; and so, doubtless also, each seaman of Nelson's fleet. Yet it will detract no whit from the admiration and reverence with which we have learned to regard Japanese valour and self-devotion, to believe that hearts beat higher and purpose stronger when Togo's words were repeated to them.

To turn now to the military deductions, which may safely be drawn from the general outline of the Japanese admiral's course, and from the time and manner of the several incidents in the prepress of the engagement, as these have so far reached us. The term "deductions" is perhaps premature, even for the very guarded inferences to which I propose to confine myself; the object of these being, as I said before, rather to direct attention and guide consideration, as further fuller reports reach us, so that the bearing of these upon naval armament may be more justly estimated.

Let it be recalled, in broad generalisation, as stated in my former article, that the Russians were superior, numerically in battleships, but decidedly inferior in armoured cruisers. The latter are practically second-class battleships, in which gun power and armoured protection have been sacrificed, in order to gain speed and coal capacity. In torpedo vessels also the Japanese were superior, in the proportion at least three or four to one. These are the conditions of respective material force, which before the meeting were qualified by uncertainty as to the relative capacity of the opposing officers and men. Prepossession undoubtedly here favoured the Japanese, and justly, as the result has shown; but antecedently, naval officers at least knew that much ought to have been effected in the several months of passage, interrupted by long repose in unfrequented anchorages, which Rojestvenski had enjoyed.

With these antecedents, two fleets met in the eastern part of the Straits of Tsushima. The battle began by day; two separate accounts place the firing of the first gun at close to 2 p.m. The scene being in nearly the same latitude as Norfolk, therefore not far south of us our own recent observation in New York is evidence that daylight would last over five hours—from 2 to 7.30. This consideration bears directly upon the employment of torpedo vessels. Some doubtless pondered— I know I did—whether, in view of the very large number at the disposal of Japan, and her comparative weakness in battleships, Togo would hurl some of his forward in daylight, hoping to sweep off one or two of his huge adversaries, at a sacrifice which his country could support.

If, as has in some quarters been stated, the Russian admiral constituted a second column, towards the enemy, composed of lighter cruisers, he may have done so with an idea of meeting the first of an attack by torpedo vessels; sending to encounter them ships which would be quite as capable as a battleship of sinking such an assailant, and which could be better spared. The disposition, in fact, would be the correlative of the idea of a daylight attack, suggested for Togo, and should it have been adopted for such a reason by the Russian admiral, I should certainly hesitate to join in condemning the arrangement, tactically considered.

Least of all should I do so on the ground I have seen, that this lighter line was thrown into confusion, and so reached upon and confused the main battle line. There would be in such conditions nothing to cause confusion among capable and self-possessed captains. The position would be one perfectly familiar to naval history; and if the main battle line of the enemy, instead of his torpedo cruisers, came on, the exposed ships simply ran "to leeward," through the intervals of their own fleet.

So far as the accounts go, however, Togo did not at once, nor for some time, send in his torpedo vessels. Should the facts, as finally revealed, confirm this, it will show that his experience supported the naval anticipation, heretofore pretty general, that torpedo vessels should not be so exposed by daylight, even when in large numbers. Neither, in order to use them, did he wait for nightfall before engaging at all. He fell on at once, when his dispositions were matured, and his famous signal repeated. The fighting began with the guns, and so continued for two or three hours.

Possibly I may have overlooked some one of the tangle of unverified details which so far constitute our *data*; but the first suggestion of a mine that I find is from the captain of the *Nakhimoff*, who reports (it is said) that 90 minutes after the firing began he felt a shock, after which the ship sank rapidly. No torpedo vessel is mentioned as nearby. The sinking of the *Borodino* is apparently attributed to gun fire, in the very full account given by the lieutenant of her forward turret; but he notes a torpedo-vessel attack towards evening, when the ship was already down in the water. The published statement of a Japanese officer corroborates the time and manner of this attack, specifically naming the *Borodino*,

Amid much vague and indeterminate mention, this so far seems the sum of the performance of the torpedo vessels by day on the first day. As regards the *Nakhimoff* her story lacks precision. Togo, indeed, reports that she was damaged by torpedo boats the succeeding night, and was found still afloat next morning. This traverses the statement attributed to her captain, and would make his quitting her precipitate; but there may be an error in names, The *Borodino* accounts are minute, and support one another.

The vessel, disabled, by several hours of concentrated gun fire—"upon which the second division had been concentrating its fire"—receives the *coup de grâce* by torpedo attack; "the fifth destroyer flotilla advance signalling, 'We are going to give the last thrust at them.'"

I remember such a probable succession of events predicted by a lecturer at our Naval War College 18 years ago; not that sagacity was needed to detect the obvious. It always has been unlikely that torpedo vessels would by daylight attack a battleship unless disabled. Even then they would be supported by the fire of heavier ships, as in this case; for we are told here that "the cruiser *Chitose* continued its fire as our destroyers pressed forward." The analogy to the ancient fireship is here maintained throughout It was after the sun went down that the destroyers became active in attack.

It will be most interesting when we know, definitely and exactly, upon what part of the Russian order, and in what manner, Togo directed his main attack. It seems increasingly evident, reading somewhat dimly still between lines, that he struck the head of the enemy's column; for he forced it to change course, and the *Borodino*, which suffered a heavy concentration of fire, as has been seen, seems to have been near the head. This would tend to precipitate the confusion into which the Russians fell, and would bear out Nelson's counsel, which the exigencies of space crowded from my last article in *Collier's*, "Outmanoeuvre a Russian by attacking the head of his line, and so induce confusion."

Into such disorder the Russians fell, facilitating still further the concentration of enemies upon separated vessels, or groups; an opportunity which the Japanese were enabled to improve by being numerically much superior in armoured vessels on the whole, though with fewer battleships. Indeed, the larger numbers of the Japanese increased much their ability to combine to advantage; for the possibility of combination increases with numbers. This if accurately inferred from the instance before us, sounds again the warning, continually repeated, but in vain, that in distributing fleet tonnage regard must be had to numbers quite as really as to the size of the individual ship

This, I say, while fully conscious of the paradox, that an amount of power developed in a single ship is more efficient than the same amount in two. In part, the present Japanese success has been the triumph of greater numbers, skilfully combined, over superior individual ship power, too concentrated for flexibility of movement.

Confusion, once initiated, was adroitly increased by sending torpedo vessels in large numbers across the head of the now retreating Russian column; an office for which their speed peculiarly fitted them. Thus began what is described in general terms as an. enveloping movement. For a body of vessels already shaken in their formation and morale to advance with falling night into a host of dreaded torpedo-boats was well calculated to increase disorder, which, when existing in the van tends rapidly to propagate itself in the rear vessels as they crowd up towards their predecessors; a circumstance that doubtless inspired Nelson's saying.

Many of us can recall what befell when the leading ship of Farragut's column at Mobile was smitten with the dread of a torpedo line. In the Battle of the Japan Sea, approaching night now gave the torpedo craft their double opportunity—the cover of darkness, and an enemy crippled and broken. Yet, although we may be sure they did much good work, the testimony more and more seems to show that the decisive effect had been produced by the guns, and that the destroyers acted mainly the part of cavalry, rounding up and completing the destruction of a foe already decisively routed.

It may be believed that they in many cases sank what the Japanese, in Nelson's phrase, might have considered already "their own ships," It is reported that this enveloping movement was shared also by some of the armoured vessels, moving by the rear, and seemingly also to the other side; a distribution of vessels and combination of movement—corresponding to analysis and synthesis—which is only possible to numbers, and enforces again the need for numbers, as well as for individual power.

What followed was distinctly of the nature of pursuit; a disorganised enemy chased, driven asunder, beaten down and captured in detail. Of the several partial encounters, incident to this characteristic action of the succeeding two days, Admiral Togo's several numbered despatches have made brief mention. In a summary of this kind they require none. It is sufficient here to note the general fidelity to the well-worn military maxim, that a flying foe must not be let go while there remains a fraction of his force which might be overtaken. The Japanese have deserved the fulness of their triumph.

★★★★★★

With these words, I take leave of Admiral Togo for the present. The time will come when we shall know more of the secret history of this war than we know at present, and more, consequently, of the man that has done so much on the sea to enhance the glories of Japan. He has already added another chapter to the history of his achievements, in the operations subsequent to the battle of the Japan Sea around Vladivostok and the Siberian littoral,—a chapter which in due course of time will be written by newspaper men, chroniclers and historians. For the present let it suffice me to have given to the English speaking public, a sketch, however rapid and incomplete of one of the warrior heroes whom Japan has given to the world in the early years of the 20th Century.

明治三十八年八月廿二日印刷

明治三十八年八月廿五日發行

著 作 者　　　　アーサー.ロイド

發 行 兼
印 刷 者　　　　金港堂書籍株式會社
　　　　　　　　東京市日本橋區本町三丁目十七番地

同 社 長
代 表 者　　　　原　亮　一　郎
　　　　　　　　東京市下谷區龍泉寺町四百十四番地

印 刷 所　　　　立 敎 學 院 活 版 部
　　　　　　　　東京市京橋區築地明石町六十番地

賣 捌 所　　　　各 府 縣 特 約 販 賣 所

（英文東鄉大將傳）
定價金七十五錢

The Naval Battles of the Russo–Japanese War

Admiral Togo.

Vice-Admiral Uriu.

Captain Togo.

Contents

Preface

Captain Togo, the author of this book, is a nephew of Admiral Togo whose fame has reverberated through the whole world, and whom all our navy respects as a gallant man of arms.

The captain took an active part in all the naval engagements of the late Russo-Japanese War, during which he kept a diary, noting down all his movements and observations and interpolating poems of his own composition; and it speaks well for the strength and loftiness of his mind that he was capable of composing poetry during such hot and exciting actions.

Making use then of this diary he wrote and published a book in Japanese entitled: *Naval Engagements of the Russo-Japanese War*, containing many facts which have never appeared in any paper or official report. The descriptions too are so vivid and realistic that the reader feels as if he were actually present at the scenes described.

The Language Association, wishing to have the book read by English speaking people abroad, obtained the author's permission to translate it, and asked me to undertake the task. Imperfect my translation may be, but I have followed the original text with the greatest closeness, and attempted to render into plain and simple English its exact meaning. For the naval terms used in the book I have consulted a few specialists as well as the author and asked for their revision; while one or two passages relating to Vice-Admiral Uriu have had his personal perusal and endorsement.

In conclusion, I wish to express my sincere indebtedness to Prof. Austin Medley and Prof. T. Murai, my colleagues at the Tokyo School of Foreign Languages for the help they gave me in my work.

J. Takakusu
Translator.
June 25th, 1907.

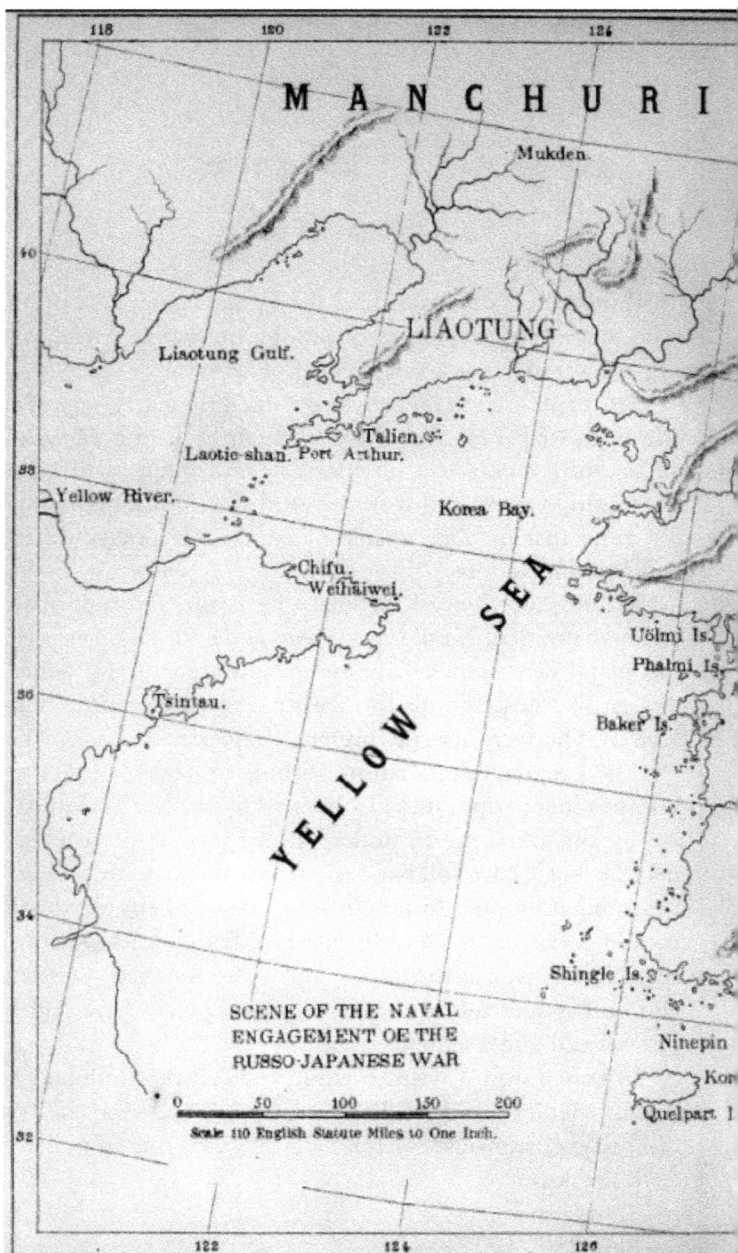

118   120   122   124

M A N C H U R I

Mukden.

LIAOTUNG

Liaotung Gulf.

40

Talien.
Laotie-shan. Port Arthur.

38

Yellow River.

Korea Bay.

Chifu.
Weihaiwei.

S E A

Uölmi Is.

Phalmi Is.

Tsintau.

Baker Is.

36

Y E L L O W

34

Shingle Is.

SCENE OF THE NAVAL
ENGAGEMENT OE THE
RUSSO-JAPANESE WAR

Ninepin

Kor

Quelpart I

32

0   50   100   150   200

Scale 110 English Statute Miles to One Inch.

122   124   126

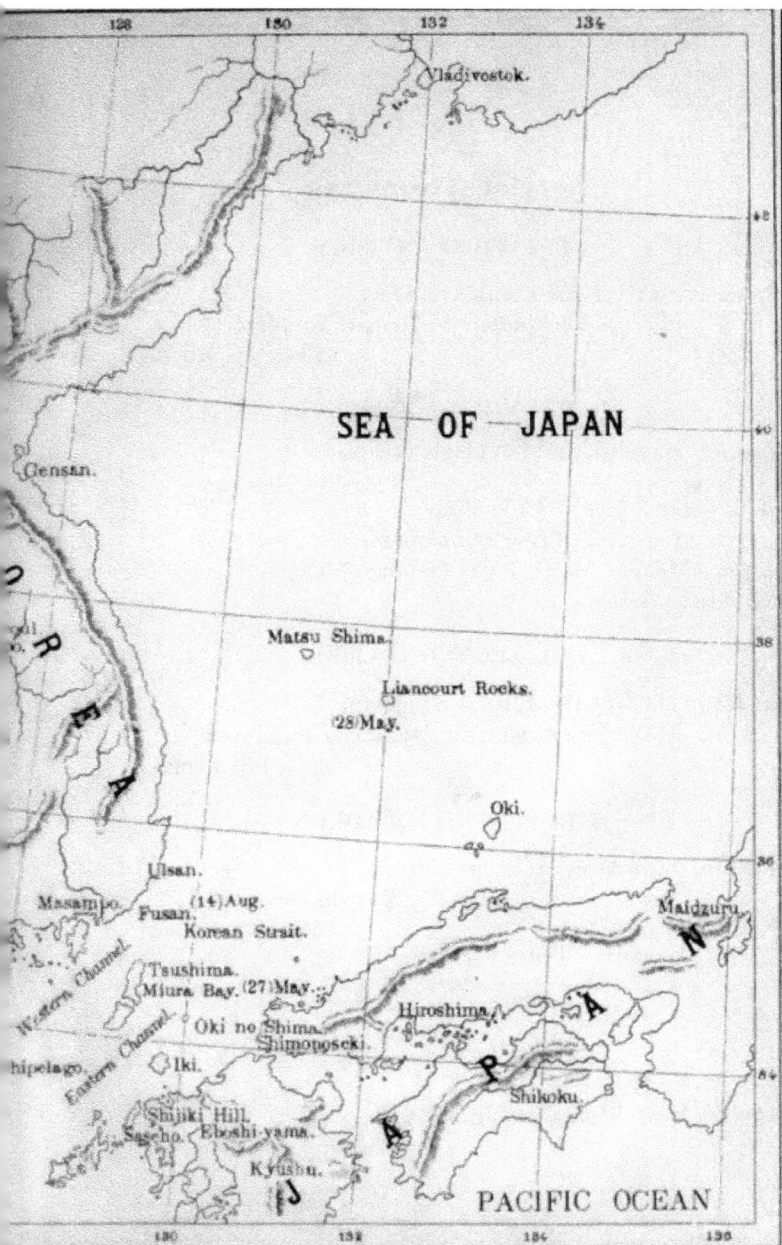

128 130 132 134

Vladivostok.

48

SEA OF JAPAN

40

Gensan.

K O R E A

Matsu Shima.

38

Liancourt Rocks.

28 May.

Oki.

36

Ulsan.

Masampo. Fusan. (14) Aug. Maidzuru

Korean Strait.

N

Tsushima.
Miura Bay. (27) May.

A

Oki no Shima. Hiroshima.

Shimoposeki.

P

hipelago. Iki.

34

Shijiki Hill. Shikoku.

Saseho. Eboshi-yama.

A

Kyushu.

J PACIFIC OCEAN

130 132 134 136

Service Formation.

THE FIRST DIVISION.

Commander-in-chief of the Combined Fleet,
Vice-Admiral Heihachiro Togo,
Flagship Mikasa.

THE FIRST SQUADRON.

In Command, Rear-Admiral Tokioki Nashiha,
Flagship Hatsuse.
Chief of the Staff,
Captain Hayao Shimamura.
Battleships: Mikasa, Asahi, Fuji, Yashima, Shikishima, and Hatsuse.
Despatch Vessel Tatsuta.

THE SECOND DIVISION.

Commander-in-chief of the Second Squadron,
Vice-Admiral Hikonojo Kamimura,
Flagship Idzumo.

THE SECOND SQUADRON.

In Command, Rear-Admiral Sotaro Misu,
Flagship Iwate.
Chief of the Staff,
Captain Tomosaburo Kato.
Armoured Cruisers: Idzumo, Yakumo, Asama, Tokiwa, and Iwate.
Despatch Vessel Chihaya.

THE THIRD DIVISION.

In Command, Rear-Admiral Shigeto Dewa,
Flagship Chitose.

Cruisers : Chitose, Kasagi, Takasago, and Yoshino.

THE FOURTH DIVISION.

In Command, Rear-Admiral Sotokichi Urin,
Flagship Naniwa.
Cruisers : Naniwa, Takachiho, Niitaka, and Akashi.

THE FIRST DESTROYER FLOTILLA.

Commandant, Captain Shojiro Asai.
Torpedo Boat Destroyers : Shirakumo, Kasumi, Asashiwo, and Akatsuki.

THE SECOND DESTROYER FLOTILLA.

Commandant, Commander Ichiro Ishida.
Torpedo Boat Destroyers : Ikadzuchi, Inadzuma, Oboro, and Akebono.

THE THIRD DESTROYER FLOTILLA.

Commandant, Commander Kokin Tsuchiya.
Torpedo Boat Destroyers : Usugumo, Shinonome, and Sazanami.

THE FOURTH DESTROYER FLOTILLA.

Commandant, Commander Gunkichi Nagai.
Torpedo Boat Destroyers : Hayatori, Harusame, Murasame, and Asagiri.

THE FIFTH DESTROYER FLOTILLA.

Commandant, Commander Iwajiro Mano.
Torpedo Boat Destroyers : Kagero, Shiranui, Murakumo, and Yugiri.

THE NINTH TORPEDO-BOAT FLOTILLA.

Commandant, Commander Junkichi Yajima.
Torpedo-boats : Aotaka, Kari, Hato, and Tsubame.

THE FOURTEENTH TORPEDO-BOAT FLOTILLA.

Commandant, Lieutenant Commander Yoshimaru Sakurai.
Torpedo-boats : Manadzuru, Chidori, Hayabusa, and Kasasagi.

I. Battle Near Phalmi (Hachibito) Island.

THE FOURTH DIVISION.

In Command, Real-Admiral Sotokichi Uriu,

Flagship Naniwa.

Senior Staff Officer,	Lieutenant Commander Keizaburo Moriyama
Staff Officer,	Lieutenant Shoshin Taniguchi.
Captain of the Naniwa,	Captain Kensuke Wada.
Captain of the Takachiho,	Captain Ichibei Mori.
Captain of the Niitaka,	Commander Yoshimoto Shoji.
Captain of the Akashi,	Commander Teishin Miyaji.
Captain of the Asama,	Captain Rokuro Yashiro.
Captain of the Chiyoda,	Captain Kakuichi Murakami.
Captain of the Chihaya,	Commander Masayoshi Fukui.

THE NINTH TORPEDO BOAT FLOTILLA.

Commandant, Commander Junkichi Yajima.

THE FOURTEENTH TORPEDO BOAT FLOTILLA.

Commandant, Lieutenant Commander Yoshimaru Sakurai.

II. Battle off Ulsan.

Commander-in-chief of the Second Squadron,

Vice-Admiral Hikonojo Kamimura,

Flagship Idzumo.

THE SECOND SQUADRON.

In Command, Rear-Admiral Sotaro Misu,

Flagship Iwate.

Chief of the Staff,	Captain Tomosaburo Kato.
Senior Staff Officer,	Commander Tetsutaro Sato.
Captain of the Idzumo,	Captain Sueyoshi Ijichi.
Captain of the Adzuma,	Captain Koichi Fujii.
Captain of the Tokiwa,	Captain Shigetaro Yoshimatsu.
Captain of the Iwate,	Captain Sadakuni Taketomi.

THE NINTH TORPEDO BOAT FLOTILLA.

Commandant, Commander Junkichi Yajima.

THE FOURTEENTH TORPEDO BOAT FLOTILLA.

Commandant, Commander Naoshi Kasama.

THE FOURTH DIVISION.

In Command, Vice-Admiral Sotokichi Uriu,
                              Flagship Naniwa.

Staff Officer,	Lieutenant Commander Keizaburo Moriyama
Captain of the Naniwa,	Captain Kensuke Wada.
Captain of the Takachiho,	Captain Ichiei Mori.
Captain of the Niitaka,	Commander Yoshimoto Shoji.
Captain of the Tsushima,	Commander Takehide Sento.

III. Battle of the Sea of Japan.

THE FIRST DIVISION.

Commander-in-chief of the Combined Fleet,
                  Admiral Heihachiro Togo,
                              Flagship Mikasa.

THE FIRST SQUADRON.

In Command, Vice-Admiral Sotaro Misu,
                              Flagship Nisshin.

Chief of the Staff,	Rear-Admiral Tomosaburo Kato.
Senior Staff Officer,	Commander Shinshi Akiyama.
Captain of the Mikasa,	Captain Hikojiro Ijichi.
Captain of the Shikishima,	Captain Inazo Teragaki.
Captain of the Fuji,	Captain Wa Matsumoto.
Captain of the Asahi,	Captain Komei Nomoto.
Captain of the Kasuga,	Captain Sadakichi Kato.
Captain of the Nisshin,	Captain Heitaro Takenouchi.
Captain of the Tatsuta,	Commander Bunzo Yamagata.

THE SECOND DIVISION.

Commander-in-chief of the Second Squadron,

Vice-Admiral Hikonojo Kamimura,
Flagship Idzumo.

THE SECOND SQUADRON.

In Command, Rear-Admiral Hayao Shimamura,
Flagship Iwate.

Chief of the Staff,	Captain Koichi Fujii.
Senior Staff Officer,	Commander Tetsutaro Sato.
Captain of the Idzumo,	Captain Sueyoshi Ijichi.
Captain of the Adzuma,	Captain Kakuichi Murakami.
Captain of the Tokiwa,	Captain Shigetaro Yoshimatsu.
Captain of the Yakumo,	Captain Yushin Matsumoto.
Captain of the Asama,	Captain Rokuro Yashiro.
Captain of the Iwate,	Captain Reijiro Kawashima.
Captain of the Chihaya,	Commander Rinroku Eguchi.

THE FOURTH DESTROYER FLOTILLA.

Commandant,	Commander Kwantaro Suzuki.
Captain of the Asagiri,	Lieutenant Commander Nobutaro Iida.
Captain of the Asashiwo,	Lieutenant Commander Dan-ichi Nauri.
Captain of the Shirakumo,	Lieutenant Commander Seiyu Kamada.
Captain of the Murasame,	Lieutenant Commander Kenzo Kobayashi.

THE THIRD DESTROYER FLOTILLA.

Captain of the Usugumo,	Lieutenant Commander Chukichiro Masuda

CHAPTER 1

Our Departure from Port and the Battle near Phalmi Island

At 1 a.m. on the 6th of Feb. in the 37th year of *Meiji* (1904) Admiral Togo, commander-in chief of our combined fleets, summoned all the captains and commanders of the Japanese navy on board his flagship the *Mikasa*. Standing in a dignified yet reverential attitude, he delivered to the assembled officers the Imperial commands that the Russian fleet should be defeated, and at the same time gave orders for our Fourth Squadron to leave port at 2 p.m. on that day to clear the enemy out of Chemulpo, and act as convoy for the military expedition to be sent there.

At that time, we could not know for certain whether the troops would land at Chemulpo or Asan, as we were waiting for the report of our lookout ship the *Chiyoda*. Saseho presented an aspect full of activity and interest that night. There were over a hundred of our warships and other vessels all shining with lights bright as stars. Innumerable boats were busily flying to and fro. Such a sight could not fail to inspire one with a spirit of daring and firm conviction of victory.

When the glorious dawn tinged the hill tops of Eboshiyama with light, we gazed at the familiar mountains and sea surrounding us. One night appeared to have wrought a cheerful change in them. Our chagrin and disappointment at the delay of our sailing orders were dispelled by the morning breeze now driving the belated mist of night before it. Officers and men alike went about with happy smiles on their faces, and cheerful words on their lips. At 9 a.m. the destroyer flotillas got into movement and left the harbour one after another, all the shipping manning yards and giving three *Banzais* as a parting salute. It was indeed a thrilling sight, and one I am incapable of describing.

After the departure of the destroyers, the Third Squadron weighed anchor, then the Second, then the First, and finally our squadron, the Fourth, followed suit, and set out to fulfil her allotted task.

At 1.45 p.m., our cruiser the *Naniwa* hoisted at her gaff the glorious ensign used at the Battle of the Yellow Sea in the Japan-China War.

The auspicious motto "*Bunn Hosho*"—May good fortune in war be yours—written specially for the *Naniwa* by Admiral Ito himself when chief of the Navy General Staff, was on the lips of all on board. Such was our triumphant departure from the port of Saseho; but before leaving harbour, Captain Wada gathered us all on deck to tell us of the unsatisfactory conclusion of the diplomatic negotiations with Russia, whereby war had become unavoidable. He exhorted each of us to discharge his duty to the very best of his ability for the sake of home and country, and at the close of his address we gave three hearty *Banzais* for the emperor and His Imperial Navy. Then passing between cheering vessels with all their yards manned we set out on our expedition.

Near Ihozaki we were joined by three transports, the *Tairen Maru, Heijo Maru*, and *Otaru Maru*, conveying the troops under the command of General Kogoshi.

When we saw Shijiki Hill on our starboard side our commander Rear-Admiral Uriu hoisted a signal on his flag-ship communicating his own conviction about the expedition, and his greeting to all under his command in the following words:

> We are now taking a last farewell of the *beauties of our native land*;
> I trust to your faithful loyalty for the performance of a great exploit for the sake of our country; and pray for the prosperity of all.

At 4.45 that afternoon the call to quarters was made on board, and after that the torpedo defences were put out, and by sunset the lookouts stationed at their posts.

With the calm of evening it occurred to us that our destroyers were to make an attack on Port Arthur and Talien two nights later, and we earnestly hoped they would have fine weather for their exploit, whether the Russians were outside Port Arthur or inside Talien-wan. We prayed too that the objects of our own expedition, the Russian ships in Chemulpo, would not take it into their heads to leave before our arrival. With these hopes and prayers, the day was brought to a close.

At dawn on Feb. 7th various islands of Southern Corea came in view, and the sea stretched all around blue and motionless; a sight particularly pleasing to us inasmuch as the smoothness of the water enabled our torpedo boats to keep company.

Out of the thousands of soldiers on the transports not one was sea-sick, and they might have been seen calmly enjoying the sight of the seagulls skimming the waves, and probably congratulating themselves on the seamanlike qualities they were displaying.

At 8.30 a.m. as Nine-pin Rock in S.W. Corea lay in sight on our starboard bow, we got a wireless message telling us of the capture of a Russian merchantman the *Russia*. The name of this early prize appeared to us to be a good omen, and hearty *Banzais* for the Imperial Navy burst from our lips.

By 4.30 p.m. we were close to Shingle Island, at which point a signal was flown from the flagship congratulating us in anticipation, and with it we separated from the main body of the fleet. The *Asama* joined us and we steered for Chemulpo, the *Takachiho* leading.

Almost immediately the latter vessel came to an abrupt stop, and when we took up our glasses, anxious to discover the cause, she signalled us that she had collided with a large whale. We soon perceived the water turning crimson with the blood of the wounded beast, and looked upon it as another incident to cheer us on our way.

Next morning Feb. 8th at 8 o'clock we made out to the far north Baker Island, a blue spot in the hazy distance, and on our nearer approach fell in with the *Chiyoda* on her way from Chemulpo. She reported everything unchanged there, the Russian men-of-war the *Varyag* and *Coreetz* being still in harbour there. Rear-Admiral Uriu signalled a message of thanks running:

The commander acknowledges the valuable services rendered by your captain and his subordinates.

From 12.30 noon until 2.30 p.m. we halted in Asan Bay, and then got under way, the *Chiyoda*, *Takachiho*, *Asama* and the torpedo boats to enter Chemulpo with the transports, while the *Naniwa*, *Niitaka* and *Akashi* followed to take up a position west of Phalmi Island and await eventualities.

Our leading torpedo boats met the *Coreetz* coming out of port, and she opened fire at once, whereupon our ships prepared for action and awaited their opportunity, but the Russian gave way before our superior force, and retired to the vicinity of Uölmi (Getsubito) Island.

Our leading detachment the *Chiyoda* and *Takachiho* then moved in company with the transports, and reached the berth for foreign warships, while the torpedo boats cast anchor within a suitable distance of the *Coreetz*, ready to open fire at any moment.

Disembarkation proceeded all night, and the *Naniwa*, *Akashi* and *Niitaka* steamed further up into Chemulpo to make a demonstration before the *Varyag*, after which the *Akashi* remained to cover the landing operations, and the other two retired outside the harbour.

In spite of the fact that the *Coreetz* had opened fire on us, the Russian warships behaved with the utmost unconcern; their washing was hanging out to dry, and their swinging booms out as if they were wholly indifferent to the great drama about to be enacted.

What must have been their amazement when they found we were prepared for action, our gunners coming up on deck with their gloves for loading. Perhaps, however, they did not know what to make of this.

During the night, our squadron lay in a position west of Phalmi Island outside Chemulpo, and observed the Russian attitude.

By daybreak on Feb. 9th the transports had completed the work of disembarkation, and left the port after dawn in company with their guardships.

Thereupon Rear-Admiral Uriu informed the senior Russian captain that the presence of his ships in the port was harmful to the general peace, and demanded, under threat of an attack in force, that they should leave by noon.

At the same time, he requested the captains of the English cruiser *Talbot*, the French *Pascal*, and the Italian *Elba* to shift their anchorage, promising that no attack should be delivered before 4 p.m. An American war-ship was also present, but she was further up the harbour.

At noon, an officer came from the *Talbot*, perhaps to decline the request to change anchorage on the ground that Chemulpo was a neutral port; or possibly, as the time mentioned in our ultimatum to the Russians had now expired, the latter had asked for the friendly offices of the foreign captains.

The enemy, however, were without means of escape from their dilemma. If they dared to engage us, their own destruction would be the result, and on the other hand retreat was impossible.

The time for decision was passing, and to safeguard their honour they seem to have been forced to resolve on fighting.

The *Varyag* and *Coreetz* accordingly weighed anchor at noon, and advanced towards our superior force with a boldness which elicited our heartiest admiration. The decision of the captain of the *Varyag*, besides being deserving of all honour, was a great stroke of good fortune for us, in that it enabled the Fourth Squadron to make a glorious name for itself. Chemulpo was a neutral port where the presence of the foreign men-of-war prevented our opening fire, and was also a very inconvenient place to fight an action in. When therefore the enemy came out to meet us, everyone was delighted. We were all grateful for the opportunity of winning renown, but the greater part of the credit attaching to the action is due to the men who served the guns on board the *Asama*.

At 12.22 precisely the *Asama* opened fire with her forward 8 inch gun, to which the *Varyag* replied.

The English officer, who was still on board the *Naniwa*, then hurriedly left in the steam launch, and all the Japanese ships went forthwith into action. The *Asama*, alone, led and was followed by the *Chiyoda*, *Naniwa* and *Niitaka*, whilst the *Takachiho* and *Akashi* formed the third firing line.

At 12.24 our whole squadron opened fire with the port battery on the *Varyag* lying about three points on our port bow, and the action lasted some 40 minutes, during which time we manoeuvred in the narrow channel. At 12.37 a shell from the *Asama* hit the fore-bridge cf the *Varyag*, and was followed by several straight shots, while three minutes later the *Naniwa* again hit the same vessel, this time amidships.

In the meantime, the Russians continued to pour in a rapid fire, but their gunnery was very inferior, some of their shots flying high overhead, others dropping short into the sea and incommoding nobody but the fish. Our shells, on the contrary, even when they fell short of the mark, burst in a most terrifying manner, while the effect of the straight shots was incredible except to an eyewitness of the dense black smoke they spread around them, and their tremendous explosive power.

At 12.55 fire broke out in the after part of the *Varyag* and she seemed trying to make for the shelter of Phalmi Island. At this sight, our men could not refrain from shouting *Banzai* and one sailor rushed into the forward battery bawling "*Zama miyagare!*"—there you are, you fools! Many of us laughed at his outburst, but after all did not that one voice express the natural indignation of Japan against ten years of Russian violence and injustice? The enemy took refuge behind the island, out of range, and we then at 1.15 ceased fire, and the action came to an end. Shortly afterwards the *Varyag* made for the Chemulpo anchorage. The Asama started in pursuit, but did not continue the chase, returning to her previous station at 1.50 p.m.

At 4.30 there was a sudden explosion accompanied by a violent shock, and a column of white smoke rose high into the air above the harbour, evidently caused by the blowing up of a Russian warship. Bringing our glasses to bear, we made out the *Varyag* lying near Uölmi Island in a half-shattered condition, and with a heavy list to port.

Not being able to see the *Coreetz*, we came to the conclusion she had probably destroyed and sunk herself, and the *Akashi* and *Manadzuru* were forthwith despatched to make a reconnaissance of the harbour. At 5.50 we received a wireless message from the former, on her return from Chemulpo, to say that they could find no traces of the *Coreetz* which was probably sunk, and that the *Varyag* was still burning, heavily inclined to the port side. We had no farther report as to the damage done to the *Varyag*, but could see through the glasses that the after bridge was all twisted up, and the fore-bridge practically wrecked.

At 6.30 we noticed a fire break out in the direction of Chemulpo, and then the sound of an explosion reached our ears, by which we understood that the *Varyag* had resorted to the last alternative of destroying and sinking herself.

Sunset on this memorable 9th of Feb. was approaching. Our Fourth Squadron had amply discharged its task of covering the landing of the troops, and destroying the hostile ships at Chemulpo, and we had passed scatheless through the first stage of the war.

Full of admiration for the illustrious virtues of His Majesty the Emperor, to which this happy result was due, all our officers and men gave vent to exultant *Banzais* for His Majesty the *generalissimo*, the whole Imperial Navy and our commandant Rear-Admiral Uriu. In the evening our staff officer Moriyama went to Chemulpo to telegraph home the report of our engagement, by which time the town was already occupied and guarded by our army, the wharf being secured with a sufficient force.

The town was full of excitement at the first day of war, and Moriyama forced his way through the surging crowds, and proved to be the first to despatch the news home.

Thus, the introductory scene of the first act of the Russo-Japanese war was auspiciously opened with a naval success near Phalmi Island.

The sailors on the *Coreetz* boarded the Russian merchantman *Sungary*. The latter, however, sustained a severe shock at the time of the former's explosion, and was in a leaky condition, whereupon they landed on Uölmi Island, and shortly afterwards the *Sungary* herself foundered.

The men then applied for surrender to our consul through the Russian consul, but afterwards some of them took refuge in the French man-of-war *Pascal*, falsifying their previously expressed desire for surrender, and forfeiting their integrity in a manner pitiful to think of.

The captain of the *Varyag* visited the English, French and Italian captains before the engagement, and asked them to leave Chemulpo in company with him; but his attempt to escape our cordon by this device proved vain, as the foreign officers did not fall in with his wishes. He is said to have returned to his ship very disconsolate. It was probably this rebuff, and the obligation they felt to preserve their honour in the eyes of the foreign men of war which drove the Russians into the hostile attitude they eventually took up.

The Russian casualties in the action were very heavy, and it was no unreasonable supposition on the part of the inhabitants of Chemulpo, both Japanese and foreign, that we had suffered too. As a matter of fact, not one of our ships was hit and there were no casualties whatever.

When Lieutenant Commander Moriyama mentioned the fact that evening at the Consulate, all, including Consul Kato, were incredulous; and even the naval officers, resident in the town were inclined to believe something was being concealed. The *Varyag* alone had over 100 casualties, and in view of that fact, and in spite of Moriyama's assertion, those present could not bring themselves to believe that we had escaped scot free.

Later in the evening when Moriyama was present at the congratulatory dinner in the Consulate, the consul plucked him privately by the sleeve and asked in a low voice:

Is what you tell us about no casualties really true? Perhaps you are obliged to say so because the facts may not be made public; are you not free to tell me the truth?

Our staff officer was at a loss to know how to dissipate his suspicions, and this incident may serve to show the contrast between the extent of damage on their side and on ours.

On the 16th of Feb., the Russian Envoy withdrew from Seöl, embarked on the *Pascal* and left Chemulpo for the outer sea *via* the Flying Fish Channel. This is the true story of his desertion of his post, for which he afterwards advanced the excuse that he was forcibly expelled.

Before the situation became threatening, a Ladies Red Cross Society of Chemulpo had been organised by a number of Japanese ladies headed by Mrs. Kato, the wife of the consul, with the view of nursing the Japanese wounded. As, however, there was no necessity for this work, they decided to tend the Russian wounded instead.

Dr. Wada, naval staff surgeon, and the head doctor of the Chemulpo hospital, took the lead in managing affairs, and the *Pascal* handed over for proper attention 24 of those wounded on the *Varyag*.

This was probably the first instance of the Red Cross Society working through the generous and humane hands of Japanese ladies for the benefit of Europeans.

The Russian wounded, who had been taken on board the English and Italian men-of-war, begged to be received into the care of the society, but owing to lack of adequate accommodation their request had to be refused. Those fortunate enough to be taken in were said to have been delighted with the benevolent and sympathetic care they received from the Japanese ladies, and afterwards presented a letter of thanks of which the following is a translation:—

> We, the wounded seamen of the sunken cruiser *Varyag*, who have been taken into the Japanese Hospital at Chemulpo, hereby wish to express our profound thanks for the generous and humane manner in which we have been treated by the Japanese authorities and the Red Cross nurses who relieved us. We are at the same time greatly indebted for the favours shown to us, the Russian seamen, by all the surgeons, doctors, and volunteer nurses, engaged in the above-named hospital, as well as all the Japanese residents at Chemulpo.
>
> Especially we are grateful for the great generosity with which His Excellency Rear-Admiral Uriu, in command of the Japanese Division, sent Dr. Yamamoto his chief surgeon to visit us in our distress and also for the labours of that gentleman on our behalf. We, the Russian seamen, are glad to have the honour of congratulating His Excellency Rear-Admiral Uriu, Surgeon Yamamoto, as well as all those who assisted in, or are connected with, the work of the Red Cross Hospital, and pray for their future happiness.
>
> Moreover, we owe our thanks to the volunteer nurses from Seöl, who came so far down to visit us, and showed their sym-

pathy toward us for our narrow escape with presents of clothes etc. Finally, we have greatly appreciated the trouble taken for us by all others of kind and generous heart.

According to the reports of the wounded, most of the men on the upper deck of the *Varyag* were wounded early in the day by our first straight shots, and the stokers had to act as shell bearers. On the forward bridge, there were a great many casualties, and a single shell swept away the whole strength of the six gunners on the fore deck. If they struck even a canvas the Japanese shells burst and scattered the fragments all over the deck, causing many injuries, and from time to time outbreaks of fire.

One shell struck the hand of an officer on the fore bridge and immediately exploded, shivering his body into atoms to the horror of all who saw it. On another occasion a shell burst on the upper deck, the effect of the explosion blowing two seamen off the flying bridge high into the air.

The high power of the explosive was simply astonishing; one shell hit the "top" and shattered the armour plate, a splinter of which was projected into a sailor's foot, piercing deep into the bone. It was afterwards found impossible to extract the piece and the foot had to be amputated, the completeness with which the shells burst was further demonstrated by one man having no less than 120 splinter wounds on his body.

The crew of the *Varyag* talked of the unpopularity of their commander and remarked to our officer:—

Our fellows on the *Coreetz* had wine served out before the action, so they were brave enough, and besides, none of your shells hit them. We did not get any wine, and so our courage failed us, and many therefore were hit by your fire.

The fact that they did not hesitate to ascribe their wounds to the omission of the authorities to serve out wine is a sufficient indication of the state of education among the Russian rank and file; the serving out of wine to the men to put courage into them seems a somewhat cowardly device.

Later in the war a Russian transport the *Manchuria* with 1000 soldiers on board was made a prize off Asan, and the men expressed themselves as pleased with their capture, and glad to avoid any fighting.

These incidents taken in conjunction reveal clearly enough the low morale of the Russian soldiers and sailors. the *Varyag* was hit three times in the port side amidships near the water line which gave her a list and the appearance of foundering. The steering gear, too, got out of order, and she was very near running aground on the north of Phalmi Island, but just managed to reach Chemulpo by means of the hand steering gear. It was at this juncture that she looked to us to be trying to take refuge behind the island.

Five times during the action fire broke out. Four times it was extinguished, but on the fifth occasion it started in the hold just below the captain's cabin and was not got under, continuing to burn till she reached the anchorage at Chemulpo where she was sunk.

The damage suffered by the *Varyag* was really quite remarkable. She had three big holes through her side near the larboard water line; the conning tower on the forward bridge was hit and her captain wounded at the same time. In addition, she was damaged in eleven other places in her after bridge, sides, funnels and mizzen top.

The numbers of the Russians taken into the three foreign warships were roughly as follows:—

The *Talbot*	300 including	20 wounded.
The *Pascal*	200 "	20 "
The *Elba*	120 "	10 "

The reason given for this unusual international incident was that the sailors themselves fled to the ships, but the foreign captains gave a pledge to our envoy that these men should take no further active part in the war, and declared that they would despatch them to their own territory; the English to Singapore, the French to Shanghai. The latter power, however, would probably make use of Annam. The Italians having no possessions in the East, had a great deal of trouble with the ill-starred Russians they had taken in. Their captain grumbled a little, but met with nothing more tangible than sympathy.

CHAPTER 2

A Tribute to Admiral Makaroff

On Apr. 15th 1904, a certain Japanese naval officer expressed his respectful sympathy to the spirit of Admiral Makaroff lately commanding the Russian Pacific fleet in the following words:—

When a warrior goes out to the field his life ought to be a matter of no concern to him. Death comes to all men, and knowing this, warriors ought to fight bravely, even if by so doing they lose their lives. But his is the greatest honour who sacrifices his life to the greatest advantage. Now yours was lost in no such happy circumstances. Your life was sacrificed as it were in vain, and no great honour accrued with your death. For your sake, I regret this most profoundly.

Looking to the advantage of my country I was rather pleased at the news that you had been killed at the very outset, but as a *samurai* of Japan I cannot refrain from sincerely lamenting your death. You were the most eminent naval tactician in Russia; you had the firmest will joined with the deepest knowledge. You were one of the three tactical authorities of repute in the present age; an honour which you still share with Captain Mahan of the U. S. A. and Admiral Colomb of England. The two latter have elaborately discussed the elements of sea power or principles of tactics and strategy, yet no man can tell what are their qualifications for fighting under the hottest fire, directing the phases of a battle, and commanding a great fleet. Your case is quite different.

In the Russo-Turkish war of 1877-8 you took entire charge of the torpedo attack in the Black Sea, when one moonlight night you dashed into the bay of Batoum with two boats, both equipped with torpedoes, and sunk the enemy's ships. The daring of your enterprise terrified the Turkish fleet although of superior force, and since then your name has gone out among the naval officers of the whole world as that of a brave and dauntless captain.

After that you made a thoroughly practical study of naval science of all kinds and were promoted step by step to the post of admiral, which you lately occupied. Whether in times of peace you were lacking in tact in your relations with your fellow officers or not, you were put in a subordinate position, removed from the centres of influence in the Russian Navy.

When, however, peaceful relations between Japan and Essie were broken, and Admiral Starck was defeated at Port Arthur in the first engagement, the Czar again summoned you to entrust you with the command of the defeated fleet. But it was too late, and your situation at that juncture still calls for our deepest sympathy towards you.

A few years ago, your work on naval tactics was published. Amongst other things your views on the influence of the moral element in battle, and use of the torpedo proved very instructive to us, while at the same time they forbade us to make light of the abilities of the Russian Navy. The facts, however, which have recently been forced upon our notice were contradictory to the inference we had drawn. In your work you laid down the moral qualifications for warriors as follows:—(1) Intelligence never hesitating at the solution of any difficult problem. (2) Power of bold decision. (3) Cool judgment at the most critical moment.

The need of these moral qualifications advocated by you was well understood by the Russian officers and men; but once the guns began to fire, there were very few among them who did not hesitate at problems set them, who dared to take bold and decisive steps risking all in battle, or who had the power of cool judgment at the critical moment. As a matter of fact, the lack of these qualities was most remarkable.

On the other hand, the officers and men of the Japanese Imperial Navy were altogether disinterested in their actions during battle, and were intent on the one aim of annihilating the enemy. At the word of command, they never shrank from meeting any kind of peril whatever. They were always bold and daring, and at the same time full of judgment. Such qualities are almost congenital in the Japanese samurai, and are the secret of the glorious development of our *Bushido*. The character of the Japanese *samurai* is thus almost identical with your ideals, and perhaps while you were yet living you looked on our *Bushido* with admiration and envy.

"You used to dwell upon the necessity of the significance of a glorious death being well understood by warriors, and argued that it was all the more important among officers and men of the navy. Nevertheless, from the beginning of the war the Russian war-ships always took to flight in the time of engagement. We never saw an instance of their coming to close quarters. The fact that their destroyers never dared to try an attack on our base affords ample proof that they lacked this feeling for the glory of an honourable death. Of course, there were two or three instances of bravery on their part, but it was a forced valour.

On the whole, the Russians value their lives and fear death too much, and for that reason alone they were foiled and checkmated in the recent war. Perhaps you saw that the situation necessitated your pushing yourself to the front, and taking direct command of your subordinates so as to encourage them and spur them on to sufficient activities. Our officers and men did not need much teaching in that line. Our torpedo boats went to the attack with shouts of *Banzai*. Our sailors undertook to block the harbour mouth in the teeth of a hostile fire with the utmost coolness, and under the hottest cannonade behaved as if on parade.

All these things were exactly what you advocated. You may well have been envious of this before your death. The moral education of officers and men was a matter on which you felt most deeply. Believing with Napoleon that military success depends three fourths on the moral element and one fourth only on material conditions, you said:—

> We ought to reverence the opinions of such an authority on tactics or strategy as Napoleon. It is a well-known fact that he devoted the greatest care to fostering and maintaining the spirit of his troops. Now it is a matter of the highest importance in the navy to tend and keep up the courage of the men, which is the key to the successful accomplishment of the tasks laid upon them all from the admiral down to common seamen. Matters of diplomacy may well be entrusted to those responsible for such affairs, but the duty of inspiring the troops and of maintaining their courageous spirit must be attended to with due care and consideration by those whose duty it is to train them.

But what were your feelings when you first came to Port Arthur as commander-in-chief of the shattered fleet there, and saw that it was a mere skeleton from which the spirit was already fled. It is perfectly clear that you felt the urgent necessity of inspiring the personnel with courage, and attempted to revive and restore their spirit. At the same time, you assiduously superintended the repair of the shattered warships, and the restoration of their fighting power.

Sometimes you made tours of inspection outside the harbour on board a destroyer, and sometimes made a swoop on our fleet in a small fast ship, thus taking every possible means of quickening the warlike spirit of your officers and men.

We specially remember how at dawn on March the 10th you despatched five or six destroyers against our first destroyer flotilla, on which occasion they made such a bold fight that their sides almost touched those of our ships. This was really the outcome of your endeavours to inspire your own subordinates, and though forced to retreat back to the harbour after a signal defeat their daring elicited our hearty admiration. Such manifestations of a spirit of energy could be nothing but the product of encouragement you gave them. But for your presence their destroyers would have hibernated within the harbour, mere ornaments.

On the same day, when the first division continued the bombardment of Port Arthur from the direction of Laotieshan, our 4th Division happened to be in the offing, and you emerged from the harbour on the *Novik*, accompanied by the *Bayan*, to attack it. For a long time, we watched each other's ensigns flying at the mast heads, but the range was too great, and, to our great regret, we parted without firing a shot. Perhaps your thus devoting yourself to the inspiration of your officers and men by cruising outside the harbour, exercising in evolutions from time to time, was your preparation against the last decisive battle which you intended to fight when it could be no longer avoided. But your end came too soon.

When our 3rd Division reached the entrance to the harbour of Port Arthur on the morning of April 13th, you bore down upon us on the *Petropavlosk* at the head of a squadron of seven warships. Seeing our division fire and retreat, you entered upon an eager pursuit, but when our 1st Division was sighted a long way off you hastily turned your bows towards the harbour again. In the course of the retreat your flagship struck on a mechanical mine laid by us, and was at once blown up and sunk. You perished then with your staff, only six officers and thirty-two petty officers and men surviving the disaster. Thus, in the end your long-cherished plans and ideas proved mere bubbles. Probably you did not look upon our shrewd operations as deceitful, though most of your countrymen have hurled that unjust accusation against us. You may have been conscious that the recent failures of the Russians were due to unpreparedness on their part, and we believe you realised that the tactics of the Japanese divisions were far superior to those of yours.

As we consider the boldness of your enterprises your fate becomes even more worthy of our sympathy. Torpedoing was your favourite line, and your name as a master of the art has been renowned ever since you attacked and sunk the Turkish war-ships with torpedoes twenty-six years ago. Now, however, a torpedo laid by us caused the loss of your own life, which was more valuable than the whole fleet at Port Arthur. Your perishing thus in the sea excites our pity all the more, because you had no chance to meet death in active fighting with us, though the fate of your fleet had already been sealed.

Maybe it is an inexhaustible source of regret with you too. We can see your noble person no more. The circumstances in which you were placed rouse our deep sympathy, foeman though you were. May you rest in peace forever, though your sorrow be incurable. In Japan, then hostile to your country, you now have friends. You are truly one of the great ones of this world. We humbly offer this tribute to your spirit.

Chapter 3

The Battle off Ulsan

At 5 a.m. on Aug. 14th in the 37th year of *Meiji*, a calm clear morning, we received, apparently from the flagship *Idzumo* a wireless message that the enemy's vessels were in sight, and thereupon our ship the *Naniwa* started with all haste to join the main body of the Second Squadron.

On the way, the call to quarters was made according to the prearranged plan of action.

At 5.20 we observed streaks of smoke rising to the N.W. of our bows, and then about the same quantity on the N.N.W. of our starboard bow. The animating sight of red flashes seen through the early morning haze made it evident the two squadrons were exchanging hostile fire, but we could not yet make out which was our fleet, and which the enemy's. Within ten minutes, however, we recognized the three ships straight ahead as the enemy's vessels from Vladivostok, and set a course to join our 2nd Division, running up our ensign at 5.40, when we were about 10,000 metres off. At this juncture, the *Rossia, Gromoboi* and *Rurik* were in single column of line of battle ahead and steering a course almost parallel with ours.

By 5.45 we had approached a little nearer, and fired our first shot at the *Rurik*, which replied at once with the guns of her after battery, several of her missiles flying just over us. As, however, the distance between us increased, we ceased fire for a while, and making for the unengaged side of our 2nd Division, ordered the men to breakfast.

By 6.35 we again neared the enemy a little, and all hands resuming action quarters, we reopened fire. At this point we observed the enemy to be staggering under the severe cannonade of our 2nd Division, and their formation began to break, the *Rurik* lagging behind. At 6.42 a fierce conflagration broke out on the laggard ship, and for a while she was enveloped in clouds of black smoke, but twenty-six minutes later the flames appeared to have been got under.

During the great fire her guns never ceased working, to our deep admiration; but finally, she was unable to keep pace with her companion ships, who manoeuvred as if to afford her protection.

Both squadrons had a good turn of speed, and it was an indescribably thrilling and animating sight to watch the ever-varying movements of the parties to this fierce action, and the thousand and one ways in which they changed position, now engaging, now disengaging, threading their way in and out in a veritable dance of death.

Amidst the thunder of the guns, and the small water spouts caused by the plumping of shot into the sea, both fleets manoeuvred in the boldest and yet most delicate manner. Despite the heavy damage they had suffered, the enemy struggled valiantly for their fellow ship, and succeeded in landing a shot on to our flagship, whereupon an ominous cloud of smoke ascended from her, which made us all tremble.

At this juncture, 7.15, the movements of our 2nd Division were really superb: our shells had set the Russian flagship on fire, a sheet of flame being visible issuing from her forecastle; but enveloped in a whirlwind of fire she forged ahead, followed by the *Gromoboi*, both of them forming a column in hue ahead. Our ships formed up in a T shape and poured in a concentrated fire from the whole line; this exciting incident causing all who witnessed it to burst into hurrahs and exclamations.

We on the *Naniwa* always did our best to avoid hampering the operations of the Second Squadron, and whenever we came too near to the enemy, orders were given for a feeble fire so as to check their movement, whilst waiting for the fateful moment of the battle.

At 7.50 the *Takachiho* joined the line of battle, thus strengthening the 4th Division.

The *Rurik* was now undergoing the last terrible attack of the 2nd Division. Abandoned by her fellow ships, she had a slight list to the port, was a little down by the stern, and indeed seemed disabled and deprived of some of her fighting power.

Considering now at 8.30 that the time was ripe, the *Takachiho* and *Naniwa* took the decisive step of attacking her. One of our sighting shots hit her amidships and we pressed on concentrating our whole fire upon her. The *Rossia* and *Gromoboi* turned as if intending to cover the *Rurik*, but were checkmated by our 2nd Division, which met and engaged them. We on our part had quite believed the *Rurik* to be disabled, but contrary to our expectations she began to move at a speed of about 12 knots an hour, and bore down upon us still managing to keep up a continuous fire from more than 5 guns. In a short time however she fell away as though not quite under full control.

At 9.10 our two ships bore away to the starboard, and attacked at her closer quarters, and five minutes later one of her 5½ inch shells hit the forward bridge of the *Naniwa*, shattering the shield on the larboard side.

Manjiro Sakano a leading seaman, and Bunshiro Shibata, an able seaman and a gunner, met with glorious deaths while Tetsunosuke Nakamura leading seaman, and Sataro Ito ordinary seaman, were severely wounded.

Luckily for us the explosive power of the shell was very low, and no more serious casualties were caused. On the bridge, a few feet away were Admiral Uriu in command of the division and Staff Capt. Moriyama, whilst on the bridge stood our Captain Wada, and gunnery Lieutenant Kobayashi. Several splinters actually passed between the captain and the gunnery lieutenant, shivering the compass stand, and it was the greatest good fortune for Admiral Uriu and the others that no further damage was done.

From the very first, in this phase of the battle we pressed the enemy closer and closer, and the effect of our spherical shells increased with the proportionate decrease in distance, while as we reached the nearest point the precision of our fire became greater. Naturally on the other hand the accuracy of the hostile fire increased also. For instance, one of their shells hit the *Naniwa* in the mizzen mast, and a flying splinter struck my right epaulette, raising a round swelling underneath full of extravasated blood, and the size of a *go* stone. A second splinter cut through my left shoe but did not reach the foot. Another shot pierced the side of the *Takachiho* but luckily did not cause much damage, while we on the contrary had the pleasure of seeing a shot of ours crash into the mizzen mast head of one of the enemy's ships, break it off in the middle, and leave only the stump standing.

Moreover, the increasing destructiveness of our fire upset their formation, for when one of them was hit, a dense cloud of smoke would arise which had the effect of completely shrouding the ship from sight for a time. When our shells struck the side armour just by the water line they would explode with fearful force producing flashes of red fire easily seen from our ships, while the splinters, flying off into the sea, made ripples which shimmered like lightning and had a peculiar lustre. Everything taken together formed a wonderful, and even delightful sight.

By this time, the *Naniwa* and *Takachiho* had fought with the *Rurik* for over an hour and a half. Her guns were silenced by our rain of shells, and her crew began to jump overboard.

Our 2nd Division, which had turned its attention to the *Rossia* and *Gromoboi*, leaving the *Rurik* to us, was nowhere to be seen, and had evidently steamed northward in pursuit of the Russians.

At 10.5 we stopped firing altogether and perceived that the *Rurik's* flag was no longer flying, as if her powers of resistance were exhausted, and she had ceased the fire. She was considerably down by the stern, and most of her crew abandoned her, leaping into the sea, as though awaiting our aid.

As the *Naniwa* slowly approached, the Russian ship sunk deeper and deeper at the stern, and when the water reached her quarter deck, canted suddenly to the left, reared up with her nose in the air, then heeled and disappeared forever at 10.40 a.m. exactly. The dauntless way in which she sustained her fire to the last, and went to the bottom when all other means of preserving her honour were lacking, was a true warrior's deed, and one worthy of undying admiration.

The Ulsan offing which a few minutes before was the scene of a fierce battle, and echoed with the thunder of hostile guns, now returned to its normal autumn state, calm, clear and smooth; and the Russian sailors drifting on the surface of the water reminded us rather of sea-gulls enjoying the perfect liberty afforded by the ocean. A contrast indeed with the desperate and exciting scene just closed.

As soon as the *Rurik* went down, Admiral Uriu gave orders for as many of the helpless men as possible to be taken in, and the *Naniwa* and *Takachiho* set to work to rescue them with their boats, the *Niitaka*, *Tsushima*, *Chihaya* and torpedo craft joining in the work of humanity. The 2nd Division too now returned from their pursuit of the *Rossia* and *Gromoboi*. The Russian prisoners taken in on board the *Naniwa* were four officers, and 129 petty officers and men, the number rescued by all our ships reaching over 600.

When our transports the *Hitachi Maru* and *Sado Maru* were sunk by Russian warships, they cruelly fired on our soldiers who were drifting over the sea without any means of resistance, and yet our squadron saved almost all their men in the most generous manner. This we commend to the world at large as a noble piece of humanity.

CHAPTER 4

How the Rurik was Sunk off Ulsan

After Father Alexis, the Russian chaplain on board the *Rurik*, was released at Saseho he made the following statement about the Naval Battle of Ulsan:—

In the afternoon of Aug. 12th, Admiral Jessen—in command *vice* Admiral Bezobrazof sick—was commanded to emerge from Vladivostok on his flag-ship the *Rossia*, accompanied by the *Rurik* and *Gromoboi*. Each of these three ships was completely prepared for action and left the naval port of Vladivostok at 5 a.m. the next day. The squadron steamed south at the standard speed of 16 knots throughout that day. At 4 a. m. on the 14th the *Rurik* sighted four steamers coming towards us, and in a little over twenty minutes, they were recognised as the armoured cruisers *Idzumo*, *Adzuma*, *Tokiwa* and *Iwate*. The call to quarters was at once made in each of our ships, and we awaited the approach of the enemy fully prepared.

(According to a prisoner's story, in this sudden encounter some of the officers took up their action stations in their night clothes. How then can he say that they were fully prepared?)

The outer armour of the *Rurik*, except for that of the engine room, was weak, and there was a great difference between the fighting power of our two completely armoured ships, and that of the four hostile vessels. In spite of this our admiral pressed on the enemy, and challenged them to battle.

(The Japanese squadron then lay to the north and the Vladivostok squadron to the south. The latter attempted to escape northwards, but we checked their flight and they were thus forced to fight with us.)

At this juncture, the Japanese squadron bore down upon us in line abreast (We know nothing of this), while we proceeded towards them in line ahead in the order of the *Rossia, Gromoboi* and Rurik. When the distance between the two parties was reduced to about four knots, the Japanese commander-in-chief turned a little to the west: our squadron however, preserved the same course, formation and speed. The enemy turned more and more to the west and formed a single column in line ahead, in the order of the *Idzumo, Iwate, Adzuma* and *Tokiwa*. (He is mistaken here.)

A cloudless day had already dawned over the quiet ocean, when at 4.45 the enemy fired the first shot, the two squadrons steering almost parallel to each other, separated by a distance of about three knots. The battle was now opened, and we fought valiantly with our sides just opposite those of the Japanese ships, as we entered the proper range. Until 9 a.m. both squadrons made the most complicated evolutions, sometimes turning to the right, and sometimes wheeling to the left, all without the slightest disturbance of their formations, just as though they had been at their ordinary manoeuvres.

(Their measurement of time varies slightly from ours as the two squadrons had different standards).

During these four hours, the engagement became fiercer and fiercer, and the *Rurik* received innumerable shots from the enemy, but in many cases our shells hit them too.

In the first stage of the battle Lieutenant Stackelberg, (commander of the *Rurik*) fell by a shot from the enemy while in charge of the battery. He was the first of our officers to be killed, and soon after his death our senior lieutenant was killed also. At 7 a.m. Captain Oesaff was struck in the face by several splinters and fell to the ground severely wounded. No sooner did I see this than I ran down to the lower deck, and returned at once to the bridge with a dressing in my hand. the poor captain was, however, again struck by splinters from a shell which hit the bridge. His body was simply pulverised, pieces of flesh and spots of blood being all that was left.

As our commander, senior lieutenant, and captain were thus killed one after another, our torpedo Lieutenant Jeniroff took command of the whole ship in their place. Up to this time from the opening of the action our casualties had been very high.

At 9 a.m. as our squadron was about to take a port turn, the Rurik, at the rear of the column, was struck in the after part by a big shell which smashed her steering gear. The rudder remained in its place but could not be moved an inch, and the Rurik which had hitherto been steaming at full speed, now did nothing but revolve round and round in the same position.

As we were unable to follow the rest of the squadron, we tried a hand wheel, but in vain, and the water was pouring into the rudder room below the water line, which was already nearly full. The only way to extricate the ship from this difficulty was to break off the rudder, which was now immovable, and steer by means of the propeller. At the order to repair the damage, our carpenter proceeded to don a diving suit, but by way of increasing our troubles he was laid low by a shot from the enemy, which caused his instantaneous and miserable death.

Perceiving our distress to be the best time for their attack the enemy concentrated their fire upon us, and the *Rurik* now became the centre of a tornado of fire from 40 or 50 hostile guns. The *Rossia* and *Gromoboi* saw this, and turned back at once to cover us under their wing, as it were. In this way, we tried to get time for our helm repairs, but our trouble was deeper than could be cured thus.

For about half an hour our two ships, as yet undamaged, fought hard with the enemy's four, but just then the *Naniwa* and *Takachiho* came in sight and drew nearer and nearer. Seeing this new reinforcement, and realising the impossibility of saving the *Rurik*, our admiral decided to let her go. The *Gromoboi* was at once ordered to withdraw at full speed ahead and the *Rossia* steered to the north, the *Gromoboi* following her example, making off at a speed of more than twenty knots. The main force of the Japanese squadron then poured in a terrific fire on us, and at once began to pursue the fugitives.

As soon as this main force had left and ceased to direct their fire upon us, the *Naniwa* and *Takachiho* drew near and showered their shells on us with a fury that left us dumbfounded, while the four larger Japanese ships steamed north in hot pursuit of our squadron. The guns on the *Rurik* had by now been so damaged by the concentrated fire of the enemy, that more than half of them were useless; nevertheless we had to face the merciless attack of the *Naniwa* and *Takachiho*.

The scene on board became more and more miserable every moment. Our torpedo lieutenant had already fallen and lieutenant Iwanof, though still quite a young man, took command of the whole ship. Our new captain saw the uselessness of fighting with guns, and tried to take the decisive step of ramming the enemy, but the Japanese squadron manoeuvred very cleverly, and always kept astern of us, their fierce fire not giving us even a moment's respite to attend to the repair of our helm.

All the guns on board were smashed except one, but the brave lieutenant kept on firing as long as there were any shells left to be fired, and any gun fit for use. Soon the shells were exhausted, and every other means failed us together with the hope of our relief. In this extremity (It was about 11 a.m. according to his note here) we noticed the *Niitaka, Tsushima* and five Japanese torpedo boats hastening towards us.

Our new captain was a cool-headed but gallant young man, and searched once more to see if there were no gun on board fit for use. Finding nothing but dismounted guns lying helpless among the heaps of corpses, Lieutenant Iwanof commanded the ship to be blown up and sunk, and on being informed that not even a fuse was left on the ship, everything being smashed to atoms, ordered the sea valves to be opened.

At the same time, he bade the unwounded men tie up the wounded in their hammocks and throw them overboard."

(The Russian navy hammocks are so made that they may be used as substitutes for life-buoys).

This was done because they asked for their lives to be saved by any means. The work was at once put in hand, and on its completion all unwounded survivors were ordered to jump into the sea with their own hammocks. Our ship was now rapidly sinking from the after part.

At this last moment, all the unwounded officers gathered together on the bridge, and were found to consist of two engineers, Lieutenant Iwanof, a probationer (cousin to the senior lieutenant already killed) and myself, only five in all. Shortly before the ship capsized we all escaped into the sea, but the probationer was a little late in leaving and was killed by a blow from the funnel of the sinking *Rurik*.

The vessel had been sinking rapidly from her stern, and when the sea water rushed into her engine room the listed heavily to port; then the ship's bottom was seen above the surface of the water, and she foundered immediately at 2.15 p.m.

(This is a blunder in the time on his part, probably the effect of the heavy shock of prolonged and severe fighting).

The whirlpools raised on the sea by the sinking of a big warship of more than 10,000 tons were appalling. No one who witnessed the scene could ever forget it. In the meantime, our men were drifting over the sea, the majority wounded, some with their feet taken off, some wounded in the back, and others with their heads dressed. Our surviving officers and men—600 in all—raised loud and gallant cheers when they were about to be buried in the ocean with their ship.

We fought to the very last. We did our utmost. The *Rurik* was not surrendered into the enemy's hands, and thus on our part there is not the slightest shade of regret.

CHAPTER 5

The Battle of the Sea of Japan.

A quarter to five, commander; all hands on deck in fifteen minutes.

On the morning of May 27th 1905 I was thus awakened by the voice of a sentry. I jumped up immediately, and washed my face and teeth; I am a slovenly fellow, and when the ship was on the alert never took off my clothes at night, so I left my cabin at once, and indulging myself in the infinite pleasure of a pipe, went up to the bridge and collected all the officers of the watch.

When the hammocks were stowed I gave orders for all hands, seamen and carpenters, to raise the torpedo nets. Just as I gave the final instructions the officers on duty reported "all well."

At the very moment, the nets were touching the ship's sides the midshipman of the watch came running up to say that a wireless message reported the enemy in sight. It was exactly fifteen minutes past five by my watch, and the signal was already flying from the flagship ordering us to prepare to leave the port at once. The nets were stowed forthwith and everything made ready for that purpose, while part of the ship which had resumed its ordinary condition was cleared for action.

Every man on board was eager and prompt in doing his allotted duty in a way not to be imagined on ordinary days, and almost instantaneously every preparation was made against the Russian fleet for which we had waited so long.

The vedette boats and steam launches which were temporarily anchored in some place more suitable for them, received the command to join and came back at full speed, evidently considering it would be a lifelong shame to them to be behind time for this battle which was big with the fate of Japan. Their hands were ordered to come up leaving their craft at anchor near the ships.

All around us our vessels were emitting clouds of black smoke, and the fleet presented a more than usually grand appearance, which in our eyes already overwhelmed the Russians.

Soon the outermost ships began to move. The flagship *Mikasa*, which was rather late in coming up, took the lead of the column, and our fleet formed up in the order of the *Shikishima, Fuji, Asahi, Kasuga* and *Nisshin*. We proceeded out of port over a tumbling sea, and made for the Eastern Channel of the Tsushima Straits, there to annihilate the Baltic fleet at a blow.

On our way, I chanted a song of my own composition:

Sashinoboru asahi kagayaku kihoi nite,
Iza kudakanan tsuyu no adafime.
E'en as the splendour of the Rising Sun,
And raging storms dispel the morning dew,
So, shall the triumph by our vessel won
Scatter the Russian ships and all their crew.

The *Idzumo*, one of our scouts, reported to us every moment by means of wireless telegraphy the formation and course of the Russian war-ships, and by now their approach was beyond doubt. The one chance in the world had come for us, and the hearts of all officers and men beat high with joyful courage and daring.

The process of clearing for action was everywhere complete. "Let 'em come on when they like"—and our officers gathered together by the after barbette, chatting over the tobacco tray.

The commander brought out a box of cigars, with which he had been presented by H. I. H. Prince Komatsu as a gift from His Majesty, and distributed them among the officers to celebrate the victory awaiting them. First class Sub-lieutenant Morishita was the only man who did not smoke.

The commander urged him to smoke a cigar which came from such an honourable source, as it might bring him good fortune in battle, and when he insisted upon declining it, Lieutenant Hatano said chaffingly " If you don't take it gladly, perhaps you will be the first to fall today." Sad to relate this jesting prophesy proved true.

While enjoying the excellent cigars we had the pleasure of listening to the phonograph, and thus amused ourselves while awaiting the encounter with the enemy.

At this time, a strong south-westerly wind was blowing, and a high and angry sea dashed against the ships' sides causing them to roll heavily. It was not easy to open the ports even on the main deck.

Delighted though we were at the idea of meeting the enemy soon we prayed for a calmer sea. Moreover, the weather was so foggy that our limit of view was five knots. More than once in critical moments of our history storms upon the western, seas have proved helpful to Japan, the most notable instance of which was at the time of the Mongol invasion of Kyushiu in 1281. This storm was designated *Kamikaze*—the divine storm—as if it had been called up by Providence.

Now once more, strange to say, it was rough weather which forced the Russians into positions unfavourable to them from the outset of the battle. We soon passed north of Tsushima but our torpedo craft had to fall out of line, the weather being too heavy for them, and they left us to take shelter.

At 1.36 the Russian fleet showed up to the west of Okinoshima. Admiral Rodjestvensky's flagship *Kniaz Souvaroff* led the column, followed by the *Alexander III., Borodino, Orel, Osliabia*—from which flew Admiral Fölkersam's flag—*Sissoi Veliki, Navarin, Nachimoff, Nicolai I.* (on board which was Nebogatoff) *Apraxin, Senyavin,* and *Oushakoff* in the order stated. The rest could not be seen in the fog. It was really a grand fleet of warships forming a grey line from which the light blue funnels showed up in distinct contrast. It steamed towards us valiantly. The Baltic fleet of the Russian Empire which was now to contend with us in the most desperate engagement, and one momentous in its consequences to the destiny of the two nations, was equal to us in the number of the ships, superior in battleships and their main armament of twelve inch guns, but inferior in armoured cruisers and eight inch guns.

At 1.40 the flag-ship *Mikasa* changed course towards the enemy's fleet so as to check their onward progress and at the same time Admiral Togo hoisted high at the mast-head his memorable signal:—

The rise or fall of the Empire depends upon the result of this engagement; do your utmost, every one of you.

Every man and officer in the fleet read it calm and self-possessed and without a trace of heady excitement.

At 2.7 the Russians opened the ball with a brisk shower of shells, but the range being too long, most of them fell into the sea, no doubt to the surprise of the marine gods. Our fleet held on for about six minutes perfectly disciplined to proceed under the hottest fire, and at 2.13 the flagship *Mikasa* discharged the first gun. Thereafter every position we took had the one purpose in view of directing our fire on the enemy, and thus at length the curtain was raised on the naval battle so long eagerly anticipated.

What with smoking guns and belching funnels the ocean was darkened; solid pillars of water shot up where shells struck the sea, and the thunder of the cannon was deafening. The enemy's fire, however, lacked precision, and whether from nervousness due to lack of experience, or want of discipline, few of our ships sustained any damage from it. On the other hand, the accuracy of our gunners was such that the clouds of black smoke caused by our bursting shells were numberless.

As the combat deepened I left the after bridge on a tour of inspection beginning with the upper deck, and was highly pleased to observe that the gun crews were as cool as at ordinary firing practice.

After my round on the main, I descended to the lower deck, and fell in forward with a crowd of men hurriedly carrying buckets of water; a clear sign of some untoward occurrence. I was a little disturbed at this confusion, and asked what they were doing. Without ceasing work, they briefly replied, "Carrying water to the 12 inch turret." I suspected that a fire caused by the enemy's shells had broken out there, but troubled myself no further and went astern. As I was ascending to the upper deck I heard a most terrific explosion from its after part; fragments of wood and splinters of shells were scattered here and there, and the wounded men prostrated amid the havoc.

Turning my eyes starboard I saw the iron plates twisted, and bloody hands and feet and mutilated corpses lying on the deck. Not a soul was left alive. then a seaman came down from the shelter deck carrying in his arms First-class Sub-lieutenant Morishita. His subordinate officer also escorted the wounded man, which caused me to give the former a sharp reprimand. "Whose duty is it to control the fire when the group leader is killed?" As if brought to the consciousness of his own duty the young officer then ran back to his place in the battery.

It was quite natural for a young officer to leave his post on such an occasion, for it would be pretty hard for him to pay no attention to his senior thus killed in action; but the position of the battle called for stoicism from the officers.

I called out to Morishita, "Fifth Lieutenant, Fifth Lieutenant!" but received no reply. His forehead was not yet cold when I laid my hand upon it, and he still seemed to breathe faintly, so I went off to enlist stretcher men and had him sent at once to the dressing station.

I then went up to the starboard shelter deck and found the shield of the 12 pounder had been pierced by a Russian shot. I was puzzled to know where to step as the shattered deck was bestrewn with pieces of human flesh and besmeared with fresh blood, whilst mutilated hands and feet and human bowels were scattered everywhere. Calling together the unengaged men near about I ordered them to remove the remains. They all hesitated to undertake such a task, so I set the example with my own hands, upon which they followed me. It was 2.40 when all these corpses were disposed of, and the issue of the day had already been decided at the first engagement of the main forces of the two fleets.

At 3.17 our 1st Division concentrated their whole fire on the van of the enemy's main squadron, who then made a starboard turn to avoid it, and we thereupon directed the shells from our port battery straight to the point at which they changed their course, and a splendid exhibition of accurate gunnery was given.

Before this the Russian flagship *Osliabia* had a fire on board, and was seen to leave the line with her forecastle somewhat submerged. In this second combat the enemy's fleet was practically defeated, and Rodjestvensky's flagship the *Souvaroff* burst into flames and stood alone out of the line at 3.23 p.m.

After the second attack, we lost sight of the main force of the Russian fleet, which, with the exception of the flagship for a time standing alone, was enveloped in gun and coal smoke. As it was the best time to find out how many shots we had fired, I gave orders to that effect to every battery commander. Happening to see First-class Sub-lieutenant Goda I bade him give the same instructions to his lieutenant, but his answers were all beside the point. I asked him again aloud if he had been deafened by the shock of the guns, and he made no reply.

Being much displeased at this I left him but my anger changed into pity when I heard that he had the *tympanum* broken by a shot fired off close to his ear in the first engagement. Soon after this incident I took another tour of inspection through the batteries when I was unanimously greeted with "Best congratulations, Commander." And certainly, we were to be congratulated on the issue of that day's battle. Similar greetings were exchanged all over the ship; we felt as if it were New Year's Day. The next duty I undertook was to visit the wounded at the dressing station on the lower deck. Some of them who had had their throats shot through and could scarcely breathe, yet cried out faint *Banzais*, Some were unconscious with shattered arms and torn mouths, and one while his wounds were being attended to, cried out to me "Commander, I am hit."

As I turned away I could not but say to him "You are the evanescent flower of the warrior spirit in full bloom."

At 4.30 our main force defiled before the *Souvaroff* concentrating their fire upon her. As she had been half disabled and now received the whole broadside from our main division, she was at once entirely enveloped in a black mass of smoke. Great fires broke out on board, and a few minutes later we saw a fearful and ominous cloud of black smoke, whilst steam vomited forth, as if her boilers had exploded.

As I was exceedingly anxious to take a picture of this awful scene I was delighted to find someone standing near me with a camera. When I brought him up and pointed out the *Souvaroff* to him he began to take a photograph with great pride. We thought the picture would be the rarest treasure, as preserving the scene of the dire catastrophe to the flag-ship of the Baltic fleet. His joy and pride in taking it can easily be imagined. When, however, the plate was developed after the engagement we found nothing on it but the picture of the hammocks used for the protection of the bridge, for he had made a gross blunder in focussing the camera. Even the hurly-burly of fire in which we stood could not offer sufficient excuse for such a mistake; but still we could not help cheering the result and laughing at it.

At 5.8 I saw our torpedo boat destroyers rushing on to attack the *Souvaroff*, and the unlucky ship was still firing the 12 pounders from her after battery both against the destroyers and the rest of our fleet.

Up to the very end the *Souvaroff* never stopped fighting and her valour deserves our deepest admiration. When we ceased fire on board the *Asahi* a 12 pounder shot from the sinking *Souvaroff* hit our foremast and its splinters flew into the conning tower causing several casualties. Quartermaster K. Yaginuma, whilst engaged in steering inside the tower, had his right shoulder pierced by one of these splinters. Quite undismayed he held the wheel in his left hand, and asked the torpedo lieutenant standing by him to look at his shoulder. The latter turned round and inspected his wound. It was big enough to put a finger in and his face was already paling under the severity of the shock. In spite of all, however, he held on to the wheel with his left hand, keeping the ship on her course so as not to hamper her evolutions, and waited to be relieved before he went to the dressing station. A brilliant example! He merits undying admiration as the model warrior. Whether performed by friend or foe such actions deserve to be set up as honourable examples to all who follow the calling of war.

Meanwhile our division once more passed by the *Souvaroff*, delivering a heavy broadside, and then again turned towards her.

At this juncture, we saw lingering near us a Russian auxiliary cruiser the *Ural* (8278 tons) with two masts and three funnels, and directed on her the concentrated fire of the whole line of our 1st Division.

At 5.45 a generous shower of 12 inch shells caused an immediate outbreak of fire, flames and smoke spreading all over her. A funnel collapsed and one mast was broken off, to be followed by the second, and finally the second and third funnels shared the same fate. She began to settle down into the water stern first as at her launch and then vanished altogether. We all shouted with joy and clapped our hands with delight at the sight of her returning to that state when her keel was not yet laid, or in other words that of nonexistence. The scene lasted for five minutes only and she sunk at 5.50.

Steaming northwards in search of the main force of the Russian fleet we happened to find four of them to the N.W. of the *Souvaroff*, two rather close to us, two quite distant. Our division steered towards the nearer ones and carried on a running fight with them for about an hour. At 7.18 *Borodino*, the leader of the Russian column, had a great outbreak of fire with flames bursting out through her deck in a thrilling manner, and our flag-ship *Mikasa* changed her course northward, the other ships astern following in turn.

When the *Fuji* was making the turn, she fired a shell from a 12 inch gun in her after battery info the *Borodino*, which was now wrapped in flames. It was a splendid straight shot and exploded on the ship causing dense masses of smoke to arise.

Then we too turned upon her the 12 inch gun of the after battery, but seeing that the shells fell a trifle short I went astern to warn the men about the range. In the meantime, however, I was told she had blown up, and when I turned my eyes towards her saw nothing but clouds of smoke. I was unable myself to see how she foundered, and marvelled at the speed with which she sunk to the bottom. Perhaps, however, it was due to the explosion of her magazine. It was just 7.23 now. At 7.25 we had orders to withdraw from the engagement, and our division steamed northwards at sunset, when our torpedo craft and destroyers flocked around the enemy's ships, occupying the situations allotted to each for attack, and biding their proper time.

Our share in the battle of the 27th May 1905 was thus brought to a close and we had to entrust the work of night attack to our torpedo flotilla.

Winds and waves had become a little calmer, and we all gathered together and prayed for a successful issue to their attack. The Russian flagship *Souvaroff* was put *hors de combat*; the *Osliabia* had left the line in the first stage of the battle owing to a great outbreak of fire, and the *Borodino* had undoubtedly exploded and sunk. Thus, the three strongest hostile battleships were put out of action. The other ships were also seriously damaged, and the whole fleet reduced to disorder. The issue of the battle being absolutely settled we felt as if we stood in a spring garden fanned by balmy breezes.

> *Tsuyu wa mina harai tsukushite hana no ka wo,*
> *Nodoka ni sason haru no asakaze.*
> *Cool morning breezes on an April day,*
> *Dispel the gleaming dew with magic breath;*
> *Entice the scent from every budding spray,*
> *And waft it gently over all the mead.*

The sun had already sunk below the horizon which became more and more dark. To the far south we saw searchlights playing here and there, and heard the report of guns like distant thunder. Evidently our torpedo boats and destroyers had begun their attack. From 8 to 10 p.m. the sounds were audible, but as we got farther away they died out of hearing. We ourselves were busy on our own ships making preparations for the battle of the next day. Empty cartridge-cases were cleared away, provisional repairs made of the damaged places, and the bloodstains which told of our brave fellows killed were washed off.

Members of the medical corps were busy in giving proper treatment to the wounded, in examining the corpses of the killed, and all the other affairs consequent on the day's engagement.

The carpenters were engaged in making wooden coffins to contain the corpses and eight were finished that night. On examining these I considered them too short to hold the corpses. Putting myself inside one of them I found that I could not lie with my feet stretched out. When I asked them why orders were given to make these so short I was told it was because of the limited accommodation of the crematoria.

"If I be killed tomorrow, you must make a longer one for me" I said with a laugh.

After all the bodies had been examined they were put into these coffins, and their ranks and names inscribed thereon, as well as on the *ihai* (tablets), which latter were kept together in a separate room.

A number of men were appointed to keep watch all night; and by the time everything was done it was about 2.30 a.m., at which hour with the other officers and men on board I held an informal service to commemorate those who were killed in the battle.

In my capacity of commander of the *Asahi* I read the following written speech:—

In the decisive battle between the Japanese and Russian navies we have annihilated the enemy's fleet and, by the self-sacrificing efforts shown today by you all, have gained a great victory. Allow me now to lay before you a line of verse expressive of the deep admiration and respect I have conceived for your bravery.

Ada wa mina harai tsukushite tatakai no,
Arashi ni chiru zo hito no hana naru.
In that same conflict which dispersed to flight
Our foe, as by some death-fraught tempests' might
Our bravest sons, like flowers too fair to last
Were stricken by the fury of the blast.

Your gallant deeds will ever find honour among us as models for warriors bright as the morning sun in our land of *Hinode*, Accept here and now the tribute of our admiration and reverence.

Our casualties in the engagement of Feb. 27th were as follows with First-class Sub. Lieut. Morishita at the head of the list.

Killed:
Leading Seaman	Saiken Maeda.
Able Seamen	Yoshimaru Miyazawa.
	Soshichi Sasaki.
	Suketaro Mori.
	Yasutaro Yamamoto.
Ordinary Seaman	Motojiro Kawai.

Mortally wounded:
Leading Seaman	Mataichiro Ueno.
Able Seaman	Yuichiro Suzuki.

Severely wounded:
Quarter Master	Kuraji Yaginuma.
Able Seamen	Shozaburo Kurauchi.

Shinkichi Kanda.
Besides 18 cases of slight wounds, and 8 of trifling hurts.

Early on the morning of the 28th May our division in company with the second steamed towards Ullodo Island to guard against the enemy escaping northward. At 6.5 we received a wireless message from our own ships to the effect that the Russians were making for the north from the south, and at 9.49 to the south west of Takeshima we saw five of them, of whom the *Izumrod*, availing herself of her high speed, escaped, while the remaining four, the flagship *Nicholai I*, the *Orel*, *Apraxin* and *Senyavin* steamed northeast.

We bore down on them cutting them off from the south but they were not, as on the previous day, the first to open fire. As soon as we got within range we did so and pressed them hard, and still there was no resistance. On closer observation we found that every one of them was hoisting the international signals and carried no flag at all on the mast-head. The signals expressed the desire to surrender and we suspended fire at once. It was utterly beyond our expectations. We had opened fire with the strongest determination to annihilate them at once, but all in vain, for Admiral Nebogatoff surrendered with four big warships without exchanging even a single shell with us.

It really was the strangest occurrence, and we were somewhat astonished and rather disappointed for a while when the 4th and 5th Divisions came up in pursnit of these self-made prisoners, who, completely encircled by us, were drifting helplessly in our midst like so many rats in a sack, as the saying is.

The commander-in-chief of our combined fleets summoned Admiral Nebogatoff on board the flagship the *Mikasa*, and accepted his surrender as a prisoner, the above-mentioned four vessels being captured at the same time.

Orders were given me to take possession of the *Orel* and work her home at the head of certain commissioned and petty officers from the *Asahi* and *Kasuga*. After the necessary preparations had been made I boarded the *Orel* at 4 p.m. with those appointed for the job. They were as follows:

Lieutenant Commander	Hanchu Nakagawa.
Lieutenant	Shoichi Kawakami.
Lieutenant	Sadao Hatano.
Engineer	Tsutomu Yoshikawa.
First-class Sub. Lieut.	Kazuma Maeda.

First-class Sub. Lieut.	Isamu Tanaka.
First-class Sub. Lieut.	Ryotaro Kaidzu.
Second-class Sub. Lieut.	Shiro Mitsuya.
Warrant Officer	Takanosuke Fujimoto.
" "	Toichi Michioka.
Engine-room Artificer	Denjiro Hashiguchi.
" "	Shosai Moritsuka.

Besides 196 petty officers and men.

When I neared the *Orel* with this prize crew, we could see from the outside how greatly she was damaged, and at the same time realise how tremendous had been the power of our fire.

No sooner had we got on board than I had them take down the flag of the sun hoisted at the time of their surrender, and unfurl instead the ensign we had brought with us.

When the Baltic fleet left home in October of the preceding year His Majesty the Emperor of Russia accompanied by the Grand Dukes Alexei and Michael visited this ship, and standing on the after bridge gave audience to the officers and men gathered in the after part. He commanded them to avenge the memory of the *Varyag* and *Coreetz* on the Japanese, and guard the honour and glory of the Russian Navy. Now over the self-same bridge flew our national sun flag!

All the Russian seamen were preparing to leave the ship carrying their kit with them as if fully determined to surrender themselves. Her quarter deck was in great disorder and when I passed through to the fore bridge the gunnery lieutenant, who was wounded on his breast and hand, came to receive me.

He spoke a little English, and when I asked him where his captain was, replied that he was lying seriously wounded in the sick bay. To my question about the commander he answered that he had gone to the flagship *Nicholai*. Thus far we had understood each other, but this was the limit of our mutual powers. Meanwhile other officers gathered together, but all shook their heads when I asked them one by one if they spoke English. Just when I was feeling somewhat perplexed at my inability to make myself understood, Lieutenant Shinjiro Yamamoto, who was a good French scholar, visited the *Orel* on a message from the commander-in-chief. Availing myself of this good opportunity, I pointed out through him to the Russian officers, how the ship was to be transferred.

Before this, however, and as soon as we had boarded the vessel, guards had been stationed at different posts. Sentries were set over dangerous places such as magazines and so on, and a very strict watch kept all over the ship.

Moreover to our officers had been assigned respectively the care of the navigation, gunnery and torpedo departments, as well as that of the engine-room and the hull, and accompanied by the Russian officers they were engaged in the business of transference.

Next the dangerous powder and torpedo magazines were examined; scattered ammunition cleared away; the sea valves inspected by our engineers and stokers, and the engines handed over to them in such a way that no hindrance to navigation might arise. In fact the utmost precautions were taken against dangerous attempts of any kind. We also did our best to send the prisoners on board the *Asahi* and *Kasuga*. Some of these, lost to all sense of shame, were reeling about in an intoxicated condition, having evidently broken into the spirit room and stolen the liquor. Their mates had to look after many of them and consequently all their preparations for leaving the ship were slowly made. Besides not only did a high sea render embarkation in boats difficult, but also the boats themselves were too few for the proper conveyance of the prisoners. Meanwhile I began a tour of inspection accompanied by a Russian surgeon who could speak and understand English pretty well, and a messenger from our signal men.

We passed first through the ward-room where we examined the whole number of the wounded prisoners, and then went into the sick bay to visit the seriously wounded captain and other damaged officers.

The captain had been hurt by a splinter during the engagement of the 27th, when he was in the conning tower, and had been confined to his bed ever since, his head and breast dressed with the same bloodstained bandages. He was miserably pale and almost unconscious, and the surgeon accompanying me said after examining his pulse, "Probably he will not live until tomorrow morning."

Besides the captain there were four wounded officers, all of whom appeared to be slightly hurt only.

The number of casualties was returned as 20 killed and 47 wounded including petty officers and men. I thought it rather strange that the list was so small considering that the ship had suffered so severely, with about 40 holes easily visible at a glance on the outside, and an almost innumerable number inside too. On my asking how it was, they explained that as a great number of casualties occurred in the first stage of the battle, their gunners were instructed to fight the guns in the armoured turrets only, and those engaged at the other guns were all made to take shelter on the lower deck. For my part I suspected that some indeed might have taken shelter under orders, but others might have concealed themselves to avoid duty on the upper deck.

After leaving the sick bay we inspected all parts of the upper and lower decks. The high sea running since the previous night made the water rush in through the shot holes, over some parts of the deck so plentifully that we were over our shoes in it, and quilts were placed on the deck to make a raised causeway for us to pass over.

The cabins were all shattered, and scarcely any habitable rooms were to be found, except one on the starboard side in the forward part of the main deck; the ward-room and sick bay in the after part, and the admiral's and commander's cabins on the lower deck. Every spot on board appeared to have been the site of a great fire. Forward the corpses had not yet been disposed of and their disagreeable smell made us hesitate to go there.

Shells and cartridge cases were scattered about everywhere; the battered sides showed unexpected portholes, and the armour plates bore marks of the terribly destructive power of our *Shimose* power. The scene was miserable in the extreme; more especially in the middle part of the upper deck, where the vedette boats are carried; there it was really too awful to look at.

After this inspection I proceeded to the fore bridge to hear our officers' account of their examination of the parts of the ship to be transferred to us. One after another, as they completed their survey, reported that, as the Russian officers accompanying them spoke no English, they had been consequently forced to carry out their examination themselves, and in order to conclude the transfer had passed those parts that came under their own observation as all in order. Our next duty was to assign rooms to our officers and men. The commander's cabin was appointed for the use of our staff, and the Russian officers made to leave it. For our petty officers and men the admiral's cabin was selected. The uncovered forecastle was set apart as sleeping quarters for their petty officers and seamen, and as there was no cabin for the Russian officers they were ordered to stay with the wounded in the ward-room.

It is true we had now assigned the quarters, but as the water had come in and washed right over the deck we had to plant out benches or drawers on the floor of the cabins, such as the commander's, to keep our feet out of the water, and had sometimes even to resort to baling.

In the midst of all this turmoil the transhipment of the prisoners was carried out, and before sunset we had only been able to transfer 500 of them to the *Asahi* and *Kasuga*. The intelligent and obedient among them vied with one another to get on board the two ships, while those who remained behind were intoxicated, and proved themselves to be the most intractable heroes, bubbling over with nonsensical speeches, probably on account of despair having driven them to drink.

About sunset the combined fleet began to get into motion, but our engineer considered that he had too little help to manage the engines properly. We were therefore allowed as a matter of expediency to employ the prisoners, and ordered the Russian chief engineer to retain on board as many as possible of his staff.

But the instructions were not rightly understood and most of his men went over to the *Asahi*, while it was hard to find whether those remaining were stokers or not; so our men, though few in number, undertook to get the engines ready for running.

At sunset, the fleet began to move and our orders were to follow in the rear of the 1st Division in the order of the *Nicolai I., Orel* etc.

On preparing to start the engines we found, among other mischiefs, the steam-pipe valves all closed, and the safety-valves of the boilers already open, or wedged up with pieces of iron so that they could not be closed. It took some time to put this right, and even then we could not at once get the engines turning round so that we were obliged to lag behind the main squadron. In these circumstances the destroyer *Usugumo* (Lieutenant Commander Chukichiro Masuda) was sent to us to act as convoy. This was a great convenience for keeping up communication with the other ships, but we could not get much use out of it.

At 10.20 p.m. we made a trial trip with quite satisfactory results, but still there were some leaks through which steam escaped. With repeated breakdowns, we did our best to navigate astern of the main squadron, but could not work up Our speed to more than five or six knots.

At 12.5 a.m. on the 29th of May we came to a dead stop on account of certain engine troubles, and after that they recurred so frequently that we could only navigate a little over ten knots.

Suddenly at 1.45 a.m. the hull of the ship listed three or four degrees to port. When the bilge-water was examined nothing unusual was noted, but the Russian officers were afraid of her capsizing and hurried to put on their life jackets, etc. All the other prisoners shared their fears, and added much to the tumult. As this proceeding made matters worse we had to instruct and pacify them by telling them there was nothing at which to be seriously alarmed.

At 3.28 a.m. the water in the boilers sank below the safety level, and in addition, as we could have no electric light on board it was dark everywhere except in places of comparative importance where we had lighted candles stuck up to give light for the transaction of necessary business. Early in the night we had heard the distant boom of cannon, but nothing whatever could we find out about any fighting that had taken place since the previous morning. Were we to fall in with the enemy's ships at such a time, without question the prisoners would rise against us. Our only source of reliance was the *Usugumo* which kept close to us, and as a precautionary measure to guard against any sudden emergency, we distributed among our men all the rifles and ammunition we had taken possession of.

In case the ship had to be sunk or handed over to the enemy again, to lose our lives would be easy, but the much greater loss of our honour as warriors would be harder to bear. As these thoughts crowded upon me, I felt greatly distressed with anxieties not easy to recount here.

For the same reason the *Usugumo* could not be despatched to make her report before dawn, and we waited in ceaseless vigilance for the day to break.

For one thing, we wanted to find out where the water for the boilers was kept, neither could we ascertain whether there was any damage to the ship's bottom, and considered it too dangerous to open the double bottom.

Postponing our examination till after dawn, we made inquiries among the prisoners if there was any boiler water and where it was kept.

At 4.15 a.m., the *Usugumo* was sent to a certain spot to report our present plight to the flagship, and request the assistance of a tug.

On her way, she fell in with the *Asama* and told Captain Yashiro all about it. The *Asama* had several shots in her stern, and her after part was submerged four or five feet with the weight of the water she had consequently made. In spite of that she prepared to come and give us a tow, and so the *Usugumo* did not send a telegram to the flagship. However by the time the *Asama* reached us we had already prepared for navigation, and did not therefore ask for her help.

At 7.45 we found out where the water was kept and set about our trial run which proved very satisfactory. Taking into consideration the dangers arising from the water we should make through the holes in our sides when wind and sea were high, we deemed it wiser to put back to the nearest naval port which would be Maidzuru.

Our engineers and stokers had not had a wink of sleep since the night before, and some of them fainted at their posts. These were encouraged to go on with their work; and by united efforts ten boilers were started up; yet this was only sufficient to drive the ship 7 or 8 knots. Consequently, ten auxiliaries were enlisted from the common seamen, and any Russian stokers volunteering their services were accepted. Our engineer and his subordinates were thus enabled to enjoy a spell of rest in turn. Their labours were indeed arduous.

At 8.18 we began our voyage for Maidzuru, and as the *Usugumo* returned to us at 9.20 we despatched her to Oki to send important telegrams to the commander-in-chief of the combined squadrons, and of the Maidzuru Naval Station, as well as to the Minister of the Navy. At 8.35 we met the flagship *Mikasa*, and got permission to put back to Maidzuru, the Asahi and Asama accompanying us as convoy and the *Usugumo* being sent in haste to Oki to telegraph from there.

At 11.30 four wounded prisoners died and we held a funeral service, which all the guards not on watch and petty officers and men off duty were made to attend.

We had brought with us on board nothing but hard biscuits and tinned provisions, and up till now had not been able to prepare anything for our meals. Now, however, things on board were somewhat settled so that we had time to cook our food, and we made use of the galley and kitchen for that purpose. As for the victuals for the prisoners, we left the matter entirely in their own hands, and our cooking time and theirs unexpectedly clashed.

Their officers were apparently unable to get even hot water, and coming to me said that they had several wounded officers, from the captain downwards, to whom they would like to give something well cooked, but they could no longer use the galley as our rations had to be prepared there.

They begged for our sympathy towards their wounded companions and requested permission to use the kitchen after us.

They were thus quite fluent in English, while they had answered nothing but "No," when I asked them if they spoke that language.

I told them that we much sympathised with the captain and the other wounded, and that they should be allowed to use the galley within appointed hours; at which with a thousand thanks for our kindness they withdrew.

We were very much amused at their being driven by hunger to speak English after their previous repeated denials of any ability to do so, and could not help laughing at them after they had left us.

When their volunteer watch was over, bottles of wine were given to the Russian stokers who assisted our men, and they were highly pleased. It was another source of amusement to us to see them joyfully bow before us, and hug the bottles when they were served out to them at the time of their relief.

There was no necessity to employ the common seamen among the prisoners, and therefore no reason to supply them with wine. Nevertheless, the simpletons would come to the door of our officers' room, repeatedly salute with upraised hands, flatter us with unintelligible chatter in Russian, and even mimic the action of drinking wine, lifting their hands to their mouths as though they were cups. Every time these troublesome fellows came we had to scold them and drive them off.

At 8.10 Captain Jung died of his serious wounds, and the Russian officers asked me to direct them how he was to be buried. I told them that a grand funeral should be held at Maidzuru, but they all requested that he should be buried at sea. We fell in with their wishes and decided to hold the ceremony early next morning. That night one of the prisoners, a Pole, came secretly to us and said that one of the Russian engineers had attempted to open the sea valves and sink the ship. As the prisoners were in great fear of this eventuality, we examined the officer in question and confined him in a room with sentries before the door.

At the same time, stricter watch was kept over all sea valves, and every possible precaution taken to protect the magazines used for keeping powder and other dangerous materials. Any key for the sea cocks still in store was routed out and disposed of, and we took the opportunity of signalling the *Asama* and *Asahi* that a circumstance had occurred necessitating grave precautions on our part, and asking them to keep a close eye. upon us.

Captain Yashiro of the *Asama* replied that he would send more men if we wanted them; but while thanking him for his offer I declined it, informing him that there was no present necessity. While thus keeping strict watch with sentries stationed at the entrance to the.

engine-room, as well as over the sea valves and so on, every Russian engineer or stoker entering and leaving the room was stopped and examined at the point of the bayonet. Some of them accused our sentry of wounding them with his weapon, and the absence of a common language made matters worse, but on examination all their accusations proved to be ridiculous.

One of the Russian officers being, as I have stated, under confinement, a brother officer pleaded his cause with me, asserting that we were wholly mistaken in our suspicions, and asking for his release.

Later on, he presented the same petition from all the Russian officers. He said:—

We are told, he is now confined under suspicion of an attempt to open the sea valves and sink the ship. We all guarantee that he committed no such action, and beg that he may be enlarged, as we will all be responsible for his never leaving the ward-room. Let us remind you that if he had wanted to sink the ship, he would have done so before our surrender. Now we have already obeyed our admiral's orders to surrender, and it is absurd to suppose that any one of us would secretly try to sink the ship at this time of day. Don't you really think so, captain?

He proffered many other reasons in his defence, but I told him that, while quite appreciating all he had said, there were other considerations on account of which his brother officer was kept confined, and refused any further discussion as useless.

The next morning, before we entered Maidzuru, first pledging all the Russian officers to take charge of him and not allow him out of the wardroom, I set him free for the first time.

When we were told that one of the Russian officers had made such an attempt, some of the younger members of our staff got so excited that they wanted to shoot him out of hand. I, however, warned them against such an action, and said:

We must pay proper regard to the honour of the Russian officers after they have surrendered, and guard against any rash deed on our part. In everything we must be fair. I have great sympathy with this imprisoned officer. The accusation against him is almost incredible, but yet the matter entail great consequences, and we are obliged to take precautions.

Thereupon I bade my subordinate officer go and take him a bottle of wine. When Lieutenant Shoichi Kawakami with the bottle in his hand entered the room in which the prisoner was confined the latter was greatly astonished, and said with paling cheeks, "Are you come to seize me?" When therefore he found out that a present of wine had been sent him, he was pleasantly surprised and expressed his hearty thanks for our good will.

The funeral of Captain Jung was held at 7.30 a.m. on May 30th. I recollected how when Iehisa Shimadzu attacked Shoun Takahashi at the castle of Iwaya Chikuzen in the Tensho era, he invited priests to conduct the funeral with due respect. An altar was set up on which he burned incense at the funeral in honour of Shoun Takahashi. "I grieve that I was born in a warrior's family and have now to kill such a valiant general myself," said he. When every preparation had been made for the funeral, again Yoshihisa Shimadzu clasped his hands and reverently closed his eyes when his enemy's head was brought before him by Takanobu Ryuzoji. In days of old all generals treated their defeated enemies in a similar way, and our code of *Bushido* ought to be carried out in a like manner today.

Mr. Jung was a captain who fought bravely to the death for his native land, and on receipt of permission from our senior captain I ordered a flag to fly half mast, and a firing party to parade at the funeral which was attended with due respect by all our officers, petty officers and men.

The *Asama* too had a flag half-masted, and paraded all hands. How did it strike the Russian officers and men when they heard of this? We wonder.

We reached the entrance to the port of Maidzuru at noon, Admiral Hidaka, commander-in-chief of the Naval Station, coming out to welcome us in a steam-launch, while the *Asama* and *Asahi* were greeted with lively strains from the band. The *Orel* had a tug close by her side from the outside of the port in order to assist her to enter, and cast anchor safely at 1. p.m.

The Russian prisoners, officers and men 268 in all were sent to the Naval Barracks, and their wounded, 42 in number, to the hospital there.

After the officers and men from the *Asahi* and *Kasuga* had left, the *Orel* was handed over to the Chief of the Naval Reserve ships at 9 p.m. that night.

Supplementary

Official Reports.

(Issued on May 29.)

The following are the reports received from Admiral Togo, Commander-in-chief of the Combined Fleet, on the naval battle going on in the Sea of Japan since May 27:

1.

(Received, May 27, Fokenoon.)

Having received the report that the enemy's war-ships have been sighted, the Combined Fleet will immediately set out to attack and annihilate them. Weather is fine and clear, but the sea is high.

2.

(Received, May 27, Night.)

The Combined Fleet today met and gave battle to the enemy's fleet in the vicinity of Okinoshima, and defeated them, sinking at least four of their ships and inflicting serious, damages on the rest. Our fleet sustained only slight injuries.

Our destroyers and torpedo boats delivered daring attacks upon the enemy after dark.

3.

(Received, May 29, Afternoon.)

Since the 27th, the main force of our Combined Fleet has continued its pursuit of the remnant of the enemy's vessels. Encountering on the 28th, in the neighbourhood of Liancourt Rocks, a group of Russian ships consisting of the battleships *Nicholai I.* and *Orel*, the coast defence ships *Admiral Senyavin* and *General Admiral Apraxin* and the cruiser *Izumrod*, we immediately attacked them. The *Izumrod* separated herself from the rest and fled. The other four warships, however, soon surrendered. Our fleet sustained no losses.

According to the prisoners, the Russian war-vessels sunk during the engagement on the 27th were the battleships *Borodino* and *Alexander III.* the cruiser *Jemtchug*, and three other ships. Some 2000 Russians, including Rear-Admiral Nebogatoff, have been taken prisoner.

4

(Received, May 30, Afternoon.)

The naval engagement which took place from the afternoon of May 27 to May 28 inclusive, shall be styled the Naval Battle of the Sea of Japan.

5.

(Received, May 30, Afternoon.)

The main body of the Combined Fleet, as already reported in a previous telegram, surrounded and bombarded the main force of the enemy's remaining fleet near Liancourt Rocks on the afternoon of May 28. The enemy having surrendered, we suspended our bombardment and were engaged in the disposal of these ships, when at about three o'clock we sighted to the south-west of us the *Admiral Oushakoff* steaming northward. I immediately ordered the *Iwate* and *Yakumo* to pursue her. They invited her to surrender, but the advice being refused, they attacked and sank her a little past six o'clock. Over 300 of her crew were rescued.

At about five o'clock, the enemy's ship *Dmitri Donskoi* was sighted to the north-west of us. The fourth fighting detachment and the second destroyer flotilla overtook her, and fiercely attacked her until it was dark. As she was then still afloat, the destroyer flotilla attacked her during the night, but the result was unknown. The next morning, however, she was discovered by the second destroyer flotilla aground on the south-east coast of the Ullondo Island. The above-mentioned flotilla, together with the *Kasuga*, are now engaged in the disposal of the disabled Russian ship.

Toward dusk on the 28th inst., the destroyer *Sazanami* captured the enemy's destroyer *Biedovi* at the south of Ullondo. On board her were found Vice-Admiral Rodjestvensky, the Commander-in-Chief of the Russian squadron, Rear-Admiral Enquist, their staff officers and others, numbering altogether over 80. They had boarded the *Biedovi* after the flagship *Kniaz Souvaroff* was sunk during the engagement on the 27th inst. They have all been taken prisoner. The two admirals are severely wounded.

The *Chitose*, while going northward on the morning of the 28th inst., discovered a Russian destroyer and sank her.

I have also received a report from the *Niitaka* and *Murakumo* that they defeated a torpedo boat destroyer of the enemy and forced her to beach herself in the neighbourhood of Chukpyon Bay (Ullondo) at about noon on the 28th inst.

Summing up the reports so far obtained, and the statements of the prisoners of war, the Russian war-ships sunk in the engagement of the 27th and 28th, are the *Kniaz Souvaroff, Alexander III., Borodino, Dmitri Donskoi, Admiral Nachimoff, Vladimir Monomach, Jemtchug, Admiral Oushakoff*, an auxiliary cruiser, and two destroyers. The ships captured are five, namely the *Nicholai I., Orel, Admiral Apraxin, Admiral Senyavin*, and *Biedovi*. According to the prisoners of war the enemy's battleship *Osliabia* was sunk after sustaining severe damage between 3 and 4 p.m. on the 27th. They further say that the battleship *Navarin* was also sunk.

In addition to the above, the third fighting detachment reports that it observed the enemy's cruiser *Almaz* disabled and about to sink at sunset on the 27th inst. But, as there still remains some doubt about it, her fate will be reported later on after further investigations, together with the result of the attacks delivered by our destroyers and torpedo boats, about which no report has yet been received.

As for the damages sustained by the various ships of our fleet, no detailed report has yet reached me; but within the scope of my personal observation, none of our ships have received any serious damage, all of them being still engaged in operations. Nor has there been sufficient time to make investigations as to the extent of oar casualties. But I may state that there have been more than 400 officers and men killed and wounded in the first fighting detachment alone.

Lieut.-Commander H.I.H. Prince Higashi-Fushimi is safe. Rear-Admiral Misu was, however, slightly wounded during the engagement of the 27th.

6.

(Received, May 30, Afternoon.)

I consider that the report that the battleships *Osliabia* and *Navarin* were sunk is well-founded.

SUPPLEMENTARY NOTE.

It has been definitely reported that the battleship *Sissoi Veliki* was sunk on the morning of the 28th inst. The total losses of the enemy may now be stated as follows:—

SUNK.

Battleships:
Kniaz Souvaroff	(13,516 tons).
Imperator Alexander III.	(13,516 tons).
Borodino	(13,516 tons).
Osliabia	(12,674 tons).
Sissoi Veliki	(10.400 tons).
Navarin	(10,206 tons).

Cruisers:
Admiral Nachimoff	(8,524 tons).
Dmitri Donskoi	(6,200 tons).
Vladimir Monomach	(5,593 tons).
Svietlana	(3,727 tons).
Jemtchug	(3,103 tons).

Coast Defence Ship:
Admiral Oushakoff	(4,126 tons).

Specially Commissioned Vessels:
Kamtchatka	(7,207 tons).
Irtish	(7,507 tons).

Destroyers:
Three destroyers.

CAPTURED.

Battleships:
Orel	(13,516 tons).
Imperator Nicholai I.	(9,594 tons).

Coast Defence Ships:
General Admiral Apraxin	(4,126 tons).
Admiral Senyavin	(4,960 tons).

Destroyer:
Biedovi	(350 tons).

Thus the enemy's total losses may be classified as follows:—

	Sunk.	Captured.	Total.
Battleship	6	2	8
Cruisers	5	—	5
Coast defence ships	1	2	3
Specially comm vessels	2	—	2
Destroyers	3	1	4
Total numbers	17	5	22

Total Tonnage   153,411 tons.

In addition to the above, the cruiser *Almaz* (3,285 tons) is suspected of having been sunk.

The prisoners number more than 3000 including Vice-Admiral Rodjestvensky, Rear-Admiral Nebogatoff, and Rear-Admiral Enquist.

7

(Received, May 30, Afternoon.)

From the reports which have since poured in from the different squadrons and detachments under my command, it is now certain that the enemy's battleship *Osliabia*, having been seriously damaged in the early stage of the engagement on the 27th inst. left the fighting line and was the first to sink, at a little past three o'clock in the afternoon. As for the battleships *Sissoi Veliky* and the cruisers *Admiral Nachimoff* and *Vladimir Monomach*, in addition to the mauling they had received during the daytime, they were so severely damaged by torpedo boat attacks during night, that they lost all power of fighting and navigation; and while they were drifting about the next morning in the neighbourhood of Tsushima, were discovered by our converted cruisers *Shinano Maru, Yawata Maru, Tainan Maru, Sado Maru,* etc.

When our ships were about to capture them, they all went to the bottom. Survivors from these Russian warships, about 915 in number, were rescued and cared for on board our ships, and in private houses on the coast. It is also certain from the statement of the survivors from the battleship *Navarin*, that she sank as the result of four hits from our torpedo boats after dusk on the 27th inst.

According to a report from the commander of the *Niitaka*, the enemy's cruiser *Svietlana* was found by the *Niitaka* and *Otowa* off Chukpyon Bay on the 28th inst. at about 9 a.m., and sunk by our ships.

There are grounds for suspecting that the *Aurora* and the *Almaz* were sunk by our torpedo boats on the night of the 27th inst. In a previous report, the *Jemtchug* was included among the ships that were sunk, but as there is room for doubt, I have to withdraw my report on this matter until the completion of more accurate investigations.

Putting together what I have reported in my previous telegrams and what I have thus far submitted in the present despatch, I may say that the eight battleships, three armoured cruisers and three armoured coast defence ships, which constituted the enemy's main strength, have all been sunk or captured, and as for the second class cruisers and other ships which served as the fleet's hands and feet, they have also for the most part been destroyed. The enemy's fleet has thus been practically annihilated by this one battle.

As for the losses sustained by us, I am in a position to state that, according to later reports, no ships have been lost except the three torpedo boats, numbers 34, 35, and 69, which were sunk by the enemy's fire during the night attack of the 27th inst. The greater part of their crews were, however, picked up by their fellow boats. As for the damage received by the ships of and above the destroyer class, it is so unexpectedly slight, that none of those ships are unfit for future active service.

With regard to the casualties among our officers and men, I expected from the outset that the list would be a long one. But as a matter of fact, later reports disclose the fact that the loss has been comparatively small. The present estimate falls below 800. The reports about the killed and wounded will be at once telegraphed as they come in, so that their families may be consoled with as little delay as possible.

In the present battle which was fought with almost the entire strength of the fleet on both sides, not only was the field of operations extremely extensive, but the weather was very misty, so that even where there was no smoke of guns or coal the vision could not reach beyond five *ri* (12½ miles). It was impossible, even in daytime, to keep the operations of all the squadrons under my command within the range of my view. Moreover, the fighting continued for two days and nights, and the squadrons have pursued the scattered enemy in every direction, some of them being still engaged in various duties in connection with the completion of the battle. As for particulars of the actions of the entire forces, it will be some days before I may be able to forward detailed reports.

8.

(Received, May 31, Night.)

According to the report of the commander of the cruiser *Kasuga*, which joined the Fleet this afternoon with the survivors from the *Dmitri Donskoi* on board, the latter ceased pumping operations on the morning of the 29th and sank herself by opening her Kingston valves. Her crew landed on Ullondo Island. They included the survivors from the enemy's sunken war-ship *Osliabia* and destroyer *Vidny*. The *Vidny* took on board Vice-Admiral Rodjestvensky, commander-in-chief of the Russian Fleet, and his staff from the enemy's flagship, prior to the latter's sinking on the afternoon of the 27th.

While engaged in the work of taking in these officers, the *Vidny* was struck by a shell from one of our warships. She subsequently took in more than 200 survivors from the battleship *Osliabia*. As this rendered it difficult for her to continue her further voyage, she removed Vice-Admiral Rodjestvensky and his staff to the destroyer *Biedovi*, and then fled northward. She met the *Dmitri Donskoi* on the morning of the 28tli, removed all the members of her crew to the cruiser, and then sank herself. According to the statement of the survivors from the *Osliabia*, that vessel had her conning tower struck by a shell at the beginning of the engagement of the 27th, which killed Admiral Fölkersam.

In consequence of the severe and concentrated fire of our warships, the *Osliabia* finally sank in the midst of her fellow warships at a little past 3 p.m., the same day. According to the survivors from the *Dmitri Donskoi*, two Russian destroyers were observed to sink while the engagement was raging at noon on the 27th. If the latter statement is correct, the number of the enemy's destroyers so far reported as sunk has reached six.

9.

(Received, June 1, Afternoon.)

The detachment including the *Yakumo* and *Iwate*, which on the 30th May, having returned from the pursuit to the north, at once set out for the search to the south, has just returned (in the afternoon of June 1). The detachment thoroughly searched the neighbourhood of Torishima and also the Shanghai route, but failed to discover any of the enemy's vessels. According to the report of Rear-Admiral Shimamura, commander of the Second Squadron and on board the *Iwate*, the hostile warship *Jemtchug* was sunk almost immediately during the battle of the 27th, at 3.07 p.m. at a point 3000 metres from the Iwate, by the fierce gun fire from the latter. At that time, the *Jemtchug* was on fire and enveloped in dense smoke, which prevented other ships in our fleet from witnessing her sinking. It was for this reason the event was lately reported as doubtful.

10.

(Received, June 2, Afternoon.)

Of the enemy's specially commissioned vessels, those which were sunk during the engagement of the 27th were the auxiliary cruiser *Ural*, transport *Irtish*, repairing ship *Kamtchatka*, and another vessel. The latter was one of the two tug-boats which were following the enemy's squadron for the purpose of facilitating its coaling operations. The sinking of this vessel was reported by the prisoners. Of the enemy's ships observed at the scene of the battle at its commencement, those whose whereabout is yet unknown are the second class cruisers *Oleg* and *Aurora*, the third class cruisers *Izumrod* and *Almaz*, three specially commissioned vessels, two destroyers and one tug-boat. The rest have all been sunk or captured. Among these remnants, the *Oleg* and *Aurora* were within the range of fire from our third and fourth fighting detachment and were observed to be on fire several times. Though they may have escaped destruction, a number of days must elapse before they are able to recover their fighting power.

Admiral Togo's Report of the Battle of the Sea of Japan.

By the help of Heaven our united squadron fought with the enemy's Second and Third Squadrons on May 27 and 28, and succeeded in almost annihilating him.

When the enemy's fleet first appeared in the south seas, our squadrons, in obedience to Imperial command, adopted the strategy of awaiting him and striking at him in our home waters. We therefore concentrated our strength at the Korean Straits, and there abode his coming north. After touching for a time on the coast of Annam, he gradually moved northward, and some days before the time when he should arrive in our waters several of our guard-ships were distributed on watch in a south-easterly direction, according to plan, while the fighting squadrons made ready for battle, each anchoring at its base so as to be ready to set out immediately.

Thus, it fell out that on the 27th, at 5 a.m., the southern guard-ship *Shinano Maru* reported by wireless telegraphy:

Enemy's fleet sighted in No. 203 section. He seems to be steering for the east channel.

The whole crews of our fleet leaped to their posts; the ships weighed at once, and each squadron, proceeding in order to its appointed place, made its dispositions to receive the enemy. At 7 a.m. the guard-ship on the left wing of the inner line, the *Idzumi*, reported:

The enemy's ships are in sight. He has already reached a point twenty-five nautical miles to the north-west of Ukujima; he is advancing north-east.

The Togo (Captain Togo Masamichi) section, the Dewa section, and the cruiser squadron (which was under the direct command of Vice-Admiral Kataoka) came into touch with the enemy from 10 to 11 a.m., between Iki and Tsushima; and thereafter as far as the neighbourhood of Okinoshima, these ships, though fired on from time to time by the enemy, successfully kept in constant touch with him, and conveyed by telegraph accurate and frequent reports of his state.

Thus, though a heavy fog covered the sea, making it impossible to observe anything at a distance of over five miles, all the conditions of the enemy were as clear to us, who were thirty or forty miles distant, as though they had been under our very eyes. Long before we came in sight of him we knew that his fighting force comprised the Second and Third Baltic Squadrons, that he had seven special service ships with him, that he was marshalled in two columns line ahead, that his strongest vessels were at the head of the right column, that his special service craft followed in the rear, that his speed was about twelve knots, and that he was still advancing to the north-east.

Therefore, I was enabled to adopt the strategy of directing my main strength, at about 2 p.m., towards Okinoshima with the object of attacking the head of his left column. The main squadron, the armoured cruiser squadron, the Uriu section, and the various destroyer sections, at noon reached a point about ten nautical miles north of Okinoshima, whence, with the object of attacking the enemy's left column, they steered west, and at about 1.30 p.m. the Dewa section, the cruiser squadron, and the Togo (Captain) section, still keeping touch with the enemy, arrived one after the other and joined forces.

At 1.45 p.m., we sighted the enemy for the first time' at a distance of several miles south on our port bow. As had been expected, his right column was headed by four battleships of the *Borodino* type; his left by the *Osliabia*, the *Sissoi Veliky*, the *Navarin*, and the *Nachimoff*, after which came the *Nikolai I.* and the three coast defence vessels, forming another squadron; the *Jemtchug* and the *Izumrod* were between the two columns, and seemed to be acting as advance scouts. In the rear, obscured by the fog, we indistinctly made out the *Oleg* and the *Aurora*, with other second and third-class cruisers, forming a squadron; while the *Dmitri Donskoi*, the *Vladimir Monomach*, and the special service steamers were advancing in column of line ahead, extending to a distance of several miles.

I now ordered the whole fleet to go into action, and at 1.55 p.m. ran up this signal for all the ships in sight:

The fate of the Empire depends upon this event. Let every man do his utmost.

Shortly afterwards our main squadron headed south-west, and

made as though it would cross the enemy's course at right angles; but at five minutes past two o'clock the squadron suddenly turned east, and bore down on the head of the enemy's column in a diagonal direction. The armoured cruiser squadron followed in the rear of the main squadron, the whole forming single column line ahead. The Dewa section, the Uriu section, the cruiser squadron, and the Togo (Captain) section, in accordance with the previously arranged plan of action, steered south to attack the rear of the enemy's column. Such, at the beginning of the battle, were the dispositions on both sides.

FIGHT OF THE MAIN SQUADRON.

The head of the enemy's column, when our main squadron bore down on it, changed its course a little to starboard, and at eight minutes past two o'clock he opened fire. We did not reply for some time, but when we came within 6000 metres range concentrated a heavy fire on two of his battleships. This seemed to force him more than ever to the south-east and his two columns simultaneously changed their course by degrees to the east, thus falling into irregular columns line ahead, and moving parallel to us. The *Osliabia*, which headed the left column, was soon badly injured, burst into a fierce conflagration, and left the fighting line.

The whole of the armoured cruiser squadron was now steaming behind the main squadron in line, and the fire of both squadrons becoming more and more effective as the range decreased, the flagship *Kniaz Souvaroff* and the *Imperator Alexander III.*, which was the second in the line, caught fire and left the fighting line, so that the enemy's order became more deranged. Several of the ships following also took fire, and the smoke, carried by the westerly wind, quickly swept over the face of the sea, combining with the fog to envelop the enemy's fleet, so that our principal fighting squadrons ceased firing for a time.

On our side, also the ships had suffered more or less. The *Asama* had been struck by three shells in the stern near the water-line, her steering-gear had been injured, and she was leaking badly, so that she had to leave the fighting line; but she performed temporary repairs, and was very soon able to resume her place.

Such was the state of the main fighting forces on each side at 2.45 p.m. By this interval the result of the battle had been already decided.

Thereafter our main squadron, forcing the enemy in a southerly direction, fired on him in a leisurely manner whenever a ship could be discerned through the smoke and fog, and at 3 p.m. we were in front of his line, and shaping a nearly south-easterly course. But the enemy now suddenly headed north, and seemed about to pass northward the rear of our line. Therefore, our main squadron at once went about to port, and, with the *Nisshin* leading, steered to the north-west. The armoured cruiser squadron also, following in the main squadron's wake, changed front, and thereafter again forced the enemy southward, firing on him heavily.

At 3.7 p.m,. the *Jemtchug* came up to the rear of the armoured cruiser squadron, but was severely injured by our fire. The *Osliabia* also, which had already been put out of action, sank at ten minutes past three o'clock, and the *Kniaz Souvarqff*, which had been isolated, was injured more and more. She lost one of her masts and two smokestacks, and the whole ship, being enveloped in flame and smoke, became unmanageable, and her crew fell into confusion. The enemy's other vessels, suffering heavily, changed their course again to the east. Our main squadron now altered its direction sixteen points to starboard, and, the armoured cruiser squadron following, pursued the retreating enemy, injuring a constantly heavier fire on him, and discharging torpedoes also whenever occasion offered.

Until 4.45 p.m. there was no special change in the condition of the principal fight. The enemy was constantly pressed south, and the firing continued.

What deserves to be specially recounted here is the conduct of the destroyer *Chihaya* and of the Hirose destroyer section at 3.40 p.m., as well as that of the Sudzuki destroyer section at 4.45p.m. These bravely fired torpedoes at the flagship *Souvaroff*. The result was not clear in the case of the first-named boats, but a torpedo discharged by the last-named section hit the *Souvaroff* astern on the port side, and after a time she was seen to list some 10 degrees. In those two attacks the *Shiranui*, of the Hirose section, and the *Asashio*, of the Sudzuki section, being each hit once by shells from ships in the neighbourhood, fell into some danger, but both happily escaped.

At 4.40 p.m. the enemy apparently abandoned the attempt to seek an avenue of escape northward, for he headed south and seemed inclined to fly in that direction. Accordingly our chief fighting force, with the armoured cruiser squadron in advance, went in pursuit, but lost him after a time in the smoke and fog. Steaming south for about eight miles, we fired leisurely on a second-class cruiser of the enemy's and some special service steamers which we passed on our starboard, and at 5.30 p.m. our main squadron turned northward again in search of the enemy's principal force, while the armoured cruiser squadron, proceeding to the south-west, attacked the enemy's cruisers. Thereafter until nightfall these two squadrons followed different routes and did not again sight each other.

At 5.40 p.m., the main squadron fired once upon the enemy's special service steamer *Ural*, which was near by the port side, and immediately sank her. Then as the squadron was steaming north in search of the enemy, it sighted on the port bow the remaining ships of his principal force, six in number, flying in a cluster to the north-east. Approaching at once, it steamed parallel to these and then renewed the fight, gradually emerging ahead of them and bearing down on their front. The enemy had steered northeast at first, but his course was gradually deflected to the west, and he finally pushed north-west.

This fight on parallel lines continued from p.m. to nightfall. The enemy suffered so heavily that his fire was much reduced, whereas our deliberate practice told more and more. A battleship of the *Alexander III.* type quickly left the fighting line and fell to the rear, and a vessel like the *Borodino*, which led the column, took fire at 6.40 p.m. and at 7.23 suddenly became enveloped in smoke and sank in an instant, the flames having probably reached her magazine. Further, the ships of the armoured cruiser squadron, which were then in the south pursuing the enemy's cruiser squadron northward, saw at 7.7 p.m. a ship like the *Borodino*, with a heavy list and in an unmanageable condition, come to the side of the *Nachimoff*, where she turned over and went to the bottom. It was subsequently ascertained from the prisoners that this was the *Alexander III.* and that the vessel which the main squadron saw sink was the *Borodino*.

It was now getting dusk, and our destroyer sections and torpedo sections gradually closed in on the enemy from the east, north and south, their preparations for attack having been already made. Therefore the main squadron ceased by degrees to press the enemy, and at 7.28 p.m. when the sun was setting, drew off to the east. I then ordered the *Tatsuta* to carry orders to the fleet that it should proceed northward and rendezvous on the following morning at the Ulneung Islands.

This was the end of the day battle on the 27th.

FIGHT OF THE DEWA, URIU, AND TOGO (CAPTAIN) SECTION AND OF THE CRUISER SQUADRON.

At 2 p.m., when the order to open the fight was given, the Dewa, Uriu, and Togo sections and the cruiser squadron, separating from the main squadron, steamed back south, keeping the enemy on the port bow. In pursuance of the strategical plan already laid down, they proceeded to menace the vessels forming the enemy's rear, namely, the special service steamers and the cruisers *Oleg, Aurora, Svietlana, Almaz, Dmitri Donskoi,* and *Vladimir Moiiomach.*

The Dewa and Uriu sections, working together in line, reached the enemy's cruiser squadron, and steaming in a direction opposite to his course, engaged him, gradually passing round his rear and emerging on his starboard where the attack was renewed on parallel courses. Then, taking advantage of their superior speed, these sections changed front at their own convenience, sometimes engaging the enemy on the port side, sometimes on the starboard. After thirty minutes of this fighting the enemy's rear section gradually fell into disorder, his special service steamers and warships scattering and losing their objective. At a little after 3 p.m. a vessel like the *Aurora* left the enemy's rank and approached our ships, but being severely injured by our heavy fire, she fell back. Again, at 3.40 p.m. three of the enemy's destroyers sallied out to attack us, but were repulsed without accomplishing anything.

The result of this combined attack by the Dewa and Uriu sections was that by 4 o'clock there had been a marked development of the situation, the enemy's rear section being thrown into complete disorder. The ships in this quarter had fallen out of their formation, all seemed to have suffered more or less injury, and some were seen to have become unmanageable.

The Uriu section, at about 4.20 p.m., seeing one of the enemy's special service steamers (probably the *Anjier*), a three-master with two smokestacks, which had become isolated, at once bore down on her and sank her. This section also fired heavily on another special service steamer, a four-master with one funnel (probably the *Iltis*), and nearly sank her.

About this time our cruiser squadron and the Togo section arriving on the scene, joined forces with the Dewa and Uriu sections, and, all working together, pursued and attacked the enemy's disordered cruiser squadron and special service steamers. While this was in progress, four of the enemy's warships (perhaps the coast defence vessels), which had been forced back by our main squadrons, came steaming south and joined his cruiser squadron. Owing to this the Uriu section and our cruiser squadron became heavily engaged with these for a time at short range, and all suffered more or less, but fortunately their injuries were not serious.

Previously to this the *Kasagi*, flagship of the Dewa section, had been hit in her port bunker below the water-line. As she made water, it became necessary for her to proceed to a place where the sea was calm in order to effect temporary repairs. Rear-Admiral Dewa himself took away the *Kasagi* and *Chitose* for that purpose, and the remaining ships of his section passed under the command of Rear-Admiral Urin. At 6 p.m. the *Kasagi* reached Aburaya Bay, and Rear-Admiral Dewa, transferring his flag to. the *Chitose*, steamed out during the night, but the *Kasagi's* repairs required so much time that she was not able to take part in the pursuit the following day. the flag-ship *Naniwa* of the Uriu section, also received a shell below the water-line astern, and at about 5.10 p.m. she had to leave the fighting line and effect temporary repairs.

Alike in the north and in the south the enemy's whole fleet was now in disorder, and had fallen into a pitiably broken condition. Therefore at 5.30 p.m. our armoured cruiser squadron separated from the main squadron, and, steaming south, attacked the enemy's cruiser squadron. At the same time the enemy, forming a group, all fled north pursued by the Uriu section, the cruiser squadron, and the Togo section. On the way, the enemy's battleship *Kniaz Souvaroff*, which had been left behind unmanageable, as well as his repair ship, *Kamchatka*, were sighted, and the cruiser squadron, with the Togo section, at once proceeded to destroy them.

At 7.10 p.m. the *Kamchatka* was sunk, and then the Fujimoto torpedo section, which accompanied the cruiser squadron, steamed out and attacked the *Souvaroff*. She made her last resistance with a small gun astern, but was finally struck by two of our torpedoes, and went down. This was at 7.20 p.m. Very shortly afterwards our ships in this part of the action received orders to rendezvous at the Ulneung Islands, and consequently we ceased fighting, and steamed to the northeast.

FIGHT OF THE DESTROYER AND TORPEDO SECTIONS.

The fight during the night of the 27th began immediately after the battle during the day had ceased. It was a vehement and most resolute attack by the various destroyer and torpedo sections.

From the morning of this day a strong southwest wind had raised a sea so high that the handling of small craft became very difficult. Perceiving this, I caused the torpedo section which accompanied my own squadron to take refuge in Miura Bay before the day fighting commenced. Towards evening the wind lost some of its force, but the sea remained very high, and the state of affairs was very unfavourable for night operations by our torpedo craft. Nevertheless, our destroyer sections and torpedo sections, fearing to lose this unique occasion for combined action, all stood out before sunset, regardless of the state of the weather, and each vying with the other to take the lead, approached the enemy.

The Fujimoto destroyer section steamed from the north, the Yajima destroyer section and the Kawase torpedo section from the northeast, bore down on the enemy's main squadron, while the rear of the same squadron was approached by the Yoshijima destroyer section from the east, and the Hirose destroyer section from the southeast. The Fukuda, Otaki, Aoyama, and Kawada torpedo sections, coming from the south, pursued the detached vessels of the enemy's main squadron, as well as the group of cruisers on a parallel line in his left rear.

Thus, as night fell these torpedo craft closed in on him from three sides. Alarmed apparently by this onset, the enemy at sunset steered off to the south-west, and seems to have then changed his course again to the east. At 8.15 p.m., the night battle was commenced by the Yajima destroyer attacking the head of the enemy's main squadron, whereafter the various sections of torpedo craft swarmed about him from every direction, and until 11 p.m. kept up a continuous attack at close quarters. From nightfall, the enemy made a desperate resistance by the aid of search-lights and the flashing of guns, but the onset overcame him he lost his formation, and fell into confusion, his vessels scattering in all directions to avoid our onslaught.

The torpedo sections pursuing, a pell-mell contest ensued, in the course of which the battleship *Sissoi Veliky* and the armoured cruisers *Admiral Nachimoff* and *Vladimir Monomach*, three ships at least, were struck by torpedoes, put out of action, and rendered unmanageable. On our side No. 69 of the Fukuda torpedo section. No. 34 of the Aoyama section, and No. 35 of the Kawada sections were all sunk by the enemy's shells during the action, while the destroyers *Harusame, Akatsuki, Ikadzuchi* and *Yugiri*, as well as the torpedo boats *Sagi*, No. 68 and No. 33, suffered more or less from gunfire or from collisions, being temporarily put out of action. The casualties also were comparatively numerous, especially in the Fukuda, Aoyama, and Kawada sections, the crews of the three torpedo boats which sank were taken off by their consorts, the *Kari*, No. 31 and No. 61.

According to statements subsequently made by prisoners, the

torpedo attack that night was indescribably fierce. The torpedo craft steamed in so rapidly and so close that it was impossible to deal with them, and they came to such short range that the warship's guns could not be depressed sufficiently to aim at them.

In addition to the above the Sudzuki destroyer section and other torpedo sections proceeded in other directions the same night to search for the enemy. On the 28th at 2 a.m. the Sudzuki section sighted two ships steaming north at a distance of some 27 miles east-northeast of Karasaki. The section immediately gave chase and sank one of the ships. Subsequent statements by prisoners rescued from her showed her to be the battleship *Navarin*, and that she was struck by two torpedoes on each side, after which she sank in a few minutes. The other torpedo sections searched in various directions all night, but accomplished nothing.

THE FIGHT ON MAY 28.

At dawn on May 28 the fog which had prevailed since the previous day lifted. The main squadron and the armoured cruiser squadron had already reached a point some 20 miles south of the Ulneung Islands, and the other sections, as well as the various torpedo craft which had been engaged in the attack during the night, gradually and by different routes drew up towards the rendezvous.

At 5.20 a.m. when I was about to form the armoured cruiser squadron info search cordon from east to west for the purpose of cutting the enemy's line of retreat, the cruiser squadron, which was advancing northward, being then about 60 miles astern, signalled that it had sighted the enemy eastwards and that several columns of smoke were observable. Shortly afterwards this squadron approached the enemy and reported that his force consisted of four battleships—two of these were subsequently found to be coast defence vessels—and two cruisers, and that it was advancing north. Without further inquiry, it became clear that these ships formed the chief body of the enemy's remaining force.

Therefore, our main squadron and armoured cruiser squadron put about, and, gradually heading east, barred the enemy's line of advance, while the Togo and Uriu sections, joining the cruiser squadron, contained him in the rear, so that by 10.30 a.m., at a point some 18 miles south of Takeshima (the Liancourt Rocks), the enemy was completely enveloped. His force consisted of the battleships *Orel* and *Nikolai I.*, the coast defence ships *Admiral Apraxin* and *Admiral Senyavin*, and the cruiser *Izumrod*, five ships in all. Another cruiser was seen far southward, but she passed out of sight.

Not only had these remnants of the enemy's fleet already sustained heavy injuries, but they were also, of course, incapable of resisting our superior force. Therefore, soon after our main squadron and armoured-cruiser squadron had opened fire on them, Rear-Admiral Nebogatoff, who commanded the enemy's ships, signalled his desire to surrender with the force under him. I accepted his surrender, and as a special measure allowed the officers to retain their swords. But the cruiser *Izumrod*, previous to this surrender, had fled southward at full speed, and, breaking through Togo's section, had then steamed east. Just then the *Chitose*, which, on her way back from Aburaya Bay, had sunk one of the enemy's destroyers *en route*, reached the scene, and, immediately changing her course, gave chase to the *Izumrod*, but failed to overtake her, and she escaped north.

Previous to this, the Uriu section, while on its way north at 7 a.m., sighted one of the enemy's ships in the west. Thereupon the *Otowa* and the *Niitaka* under the command of Captain Arima, of the former cruiser, were detached to destroy her. At 9 a.m. they drew up to her, and found that she was the *Svietlana*, accompanied by a destroyer. Pushing closer, they opened fire, and after about an hour's engagement, sank the *Svietlana* at 11. 6 a.m., off Chyukpyŏng Bay. the *Niitaka*, accompanied by the destroyer *Murakumo*, which had just arrived, continued the pursuit of the enemy's destroyer *Buistri*, and at 11.50 a.m. drove it ashore and destroyed it in an unnamed bay some five miles north of Chyukpyŏng Bay. The survivors of these two vessels were all rescued by our special service steamers *America Maru* and *Kasuga Maru*.

The main part of our combined squadron which had received the enemy's surrender were still near the place of the surrender, and engaged in dealing with the four captured ships, when, at 3 p.m. the enemy's vessel *Admiral Oushakoff* was sighted approaching from the south. A detachment consisting of the *Iwate* and the *Yakumo* was immediately sent after her, and at a little after 8 p.m. overtook her, as she steamed south. They summoned her to surrender, but for reply she opened fire, and there was nothing for it but to attack her. She was finally sunk, and her survivors, over 300, were rescued.

At 3.30 p.m., the destroyers *Sazanami* and *Kagero* sighted two hostile destroyers escaping east, and then at a point some forty miles southwest of Ulneung Islands. These were pursued at full speed to the northwest, and being overtaken at 4.45 p.m. action commenced. The rearmost of the two destroyers then ran up a white flag in token of surrender, whereupon the. *Sazanami* immediately took possession of her. She was found to be the *Biedvi* with Vice-Admiral Rodjestvensky and his staff on board. These with her crew were made prisoners. The *Kagero* meanwhile continued the chase of the other destroyer up to half-past six, but she finally escaped north.

At 5 p.m. the Uriu section and the Yajima destroyer section, which were searching for the enemy in a westerly direction, sighted the battleship *Dmitri Donskoi*, steaming north, and went in pursuit. Just as the Russian vessel had reached a point some thirty miles south of the Ulneung Islands, the *Otowa* and the *Niitaka*, with the destroyers *Asagiri*, *Shirakumo*, and *Fubuki*, which were coming back from Chyukpyöng Bay, bore down on her from the west and opened fire, so that she was brought between a cross cannonade from these and the Uriu section. This heavy fire from both sides was kept up until after sunset, by which time she was almost shattered, but still afloat.

During the night, she passed out of sight. As soon as the cruisers had ceased firing on her, the *Fubuki* and the *Yajima* destroyer section attacked her, but the result was uncertain. On the following morning, however, she was seen drifting near the south-east coast of the Ulneung Islands, where she finally sank. Her survivors who had landed on the islands, were taken off by the *Kasuga* and the *Fubuki*.

While the greater part of the combined squadrons were thus busily engaged in the north, dealing with the results of the pursuit, there were in the south also some considerable captures of ships remaining at the scene of the action. Thus the special service steamers *Shinano Maru*, *Tainan Maru*, and *Yawata Maru* which had set out early on the morning of the 28th, charged with the duty of searching the place of the engagement, sighted the *Sissoi Veliky* at a point some thirty miles north-east of Karasaki. She had been struck by torpedoes the night before, and was now on the point of sinking. They made preparations for capturing her, and took off her crew. She went down, however, at 11.6 a.m.

Again at 5.30 a.m. the destroyer *Shiranui* and special service steamer *Sado Maru* found the *Admiral Nachimoff* in a sinking condition some five miles east of Kotozaki in Tsushima. Thereafter they sighted the *Vladimir Monomach* approaching the same neighbourhood with a heavy list. The *Sado Maru* took measures for capturing both these ships, but they were so greatly shattered and were makings water so fast that they sank in succession at about 10 a.m. after their crews had been removed. Just then the enemy's destroyer *Gromky* hove in sight and suddenly steamed off northward.

The destroyer *Shiranui* went in pursuit, and about 11.30 a.m. attacked her, No. 63, a unit of the torpedo boat sections, co-operating in the attack. The enemy's fire having been silenced, the destroyer was captured and her crew were made prisoners, but her injuries were so severe that she sank at 12.43 p.m. In addition to the above, the gunboats and special service steamers of our fleet, searching the coasts in the neighbourhood after the battle, picked up not a few of the crews of the sunken ships. Including the crews of the captured vessels, the prisoners aggregated about 6000.

The above are the results of the battle which continued from the afternoon of the 27th till the afternoon of the 28th. Subsequently, a part of the fleet conducted a search far southwards, but not a sign was seen of any of the enemy's ships. About thirty-eight of his vessels had attempted to pass the Sea of Japan, and of these, the ships that I believe to have escaped destruction or capture at our hands were limited to a few cruisers, destroyers, and special service steamers. Our own losses in the two days' fight were only three torpedo boats. Some others of our vessels sustained more or less injury, but not even one of them is incapacitated for future service. Our casualties throughout the whole fleet were 116 killed and 538 wounded, officers included, as shown in the detailed list appended.

There was no great difference in the strengths of the opposing forces in this action, and I consider that the enemy's officers and men fought with the utmost energy and intrepidity on behalf of their country. If, nevertheless, our combined squadrons won the victory and achieved the remarkable success recorded above, it was because of the virtues of His Majesty the Emperor, not owing to any human prowess. It cannot but be believed that the small number of our casualties was due to the protection of the spirits of the Imperial ancestors. Even our officers and men, who fought so valiantly and so stoutly, seeing these results, could find no language to express their astonishment.

COMPARATIVE STATEMENT.—THE ENEMY'S SHIPS AND THEIR FATE.

1. Battleships, eight; whereof six were sunk (the *Kniaz Souvaroff*, the *Alexander III.*, the *Borodino*, the *Osliabia* the *Sissoi Veliky*, and the *Navarin*), and two were captured (the *Orel* and *Nikolai I.*).

2. Cruisers, nine; whereof four were sunk (the *Admiral Nachimoff*

the *Dmitri Donskoi*, the *Vladimir Monomach*, and the *Svietlana*); three fled to Manila and were interned (the *Aurora*, the *Oleg*, and the *Jemtchug*); one escaped to Vladivostok (the *Almaz*), and one became a wreck in Vladimir Bay (the *Izumrod*),

3. Coast defence ships, three; whereof one was sunk (the *Admiral Oushakoff*) and two were captured (the *Admiral Apraxin* and the *Admiral Senyavin*).

Destroyers, nine; whereof four were sunk (the *Buini*, the *Buistri*, the *Gromky*, and one other): one captured (the *Biedovi*); one went down on account of her injuries when attempting to reach Shanghai (the *Blestyaschtchi*); one fled to Shanghai and was disarmed (the *Bodri*); one escaped to Vladivostok (the *Bravi*), and the fate of one is unknown.

4. Auxiliary cruiser, one; which was sunk (the *Ural*),

5. Special service steamers, six; whereof four were sunk (the *Kamchatka* the *Iltis*, the *Anastney*, and the *Russi*); and two fled to Shanghai, where they were interned (the *Kovea* and the *Sveri*).

6. Hospital ships, two; which were both seized, one (the *Kastroma* being subsequently released, and the other (the *Orel*) made a prize of war.

RECAPITULATION. THIRTY-EIGHT SHIPS.

Twenty, sunk.

Six, captured.

Two, went to the bottom or were shattered while escaping.

Six, disarmed and interned after flight to neutral ports.

One, fate unknown.

One, released after capture.

Two, escaped.

ADMIRAL TOGO'S REPORT TO THE EMPEROR.

On the occasion of his visit to the Imperial Palace on Oct. 22nd Admiral Togo, Commander-in-Chief of the Combined Fleet, presented to His Majesty the Emperor the following report on the naval warfare:—

Since the departure of the Combined Fleet for the front, in accordance with an Imperial Order, in February of last year, one year and a half have elapsed, and during that period every battle on land and sea has resulted in victory for the Imperial Army and Navy. Today, peace being restored, we, Your Majesty's humble servants, after discharging our duties, are able to return in triumph to the capital. This is solely due to the illustrious virtues of Your Majesty, for which we are very thankful.

When the Combined Fleet commenced its first operations on the sea, acting in accordance with the Imperial order, I, in consideration of the state of affairs on land and sea, made it the object of our strategy to press the main force of the enemy's squadron in the direction of Port Arthur, and to prevent the enemy's ships from proceeding to the stronghold of Vladivostok. With this end in view we delivered immediate attacks on the enemy at Port Arthur and Chemulpo, and continued to further attack him, gradually diminishing his strength.

We also repeatedly attempted the dangerous task of blockading the enemy's port, and laid mines in front of the latter, in order to minimize the sphere within which the enemy could operate. A portion of the Fleet was stationed at a strategical point in the Corean Straits, with the object of checking the enemy at Vladivostok, and at the same time of making the straits a second line of defence against the enemy at Port Arthur.

During the first half of this period of operations, the enemy, taking advantage of the locality, always assumed the defensive, thus making our repeated attacks fruitless. Toward the middle of August, when the main force of the enemy's squadron attempted to escape from Port Arthur to Vladivostok, the battles in the Yellow Sea and off Ulsan took place. By the enemy's action during these battles, we were successful in fully understanding his plan of operations, and in accomplishing more than half of our scheme. Afterwards, the military operations against the enemy gradually improved, and the untiring efforts of our Investing army in the rear of Port Arthur, acting in co-operation with the permanent blockade at sea, finally resulted in the destruction of the main portion of the enemy's squadron at the stronghold.

Reviewing the operations during this period, we believe that our success farther increased as the war progressed, and that during this some ten months of fighting the energy and bravery of our officers were displayed to the highest degree. We further believe that in spite of the death of not a small number of our brave officers and men, and the destruction of several warships, the final result of the war was then determined, and the decisive victory in the Sea of Japan may be traced to this first period of operations.

The second period of the naval operations commenced with this year. Oar fleet reorganised its forces so as to meet the enemy's second squadron. At the same time the Russian littoral provinces were blockaded, and a detachment was occasionally sent to the southern seas in order to carry out demonstrations along the enemy's route.

During this period, the number of vessels seized at the Tsushima, Tsugaru, Soya, Kunajiri and other straits reached more than 30. In May,, as the enemy's second squadron appeared in the neighbouring waters, our entire forces were concentrated at the Corean Channel, acting on the principle of meeting an exhausted enemy by a force ready for action. By the grace of Heaven, our gallant officers and men scored successes one by one; and the enemy being swept away from the surface of the sea once and for all, by the battle of the Sea of Japan, the operations of the period were brought to a conclusion.

Since then the sea has been completely under our control in name and reality, and the third period of the naval operations opened with a great decrease in our duties. At times we assisted the army in the conquest of Karafuto, and discharged our duties of co-operation without the loss of a single life. At intervals we carried out demonstrative operations in North Corea. The blockade of the Russian provinces, on the other hand, was firmly maintained till the restoration of peace.

In short, the operations of the Combined Fleet were carried out in order to elucidate the situation in the first period, to achieve victory in the second period, and to reap the fruits of such victories in the third period. In spite of the importance and difficulty of the task the naval operations on the whole made smooth progress, find have been brought to the present conclusion. The Imperial warships which have returned to Tokyo Bay in triumph, number more than 170, including small craft. Though several vessels were lost in the war, still we have the honour to mention that our fleet, having acquired several vessels as prizes of war, retains a strength not inferior to that before the war.

In conclusion, I, Your Majesty's humble subject, appreciate the successes won by the army in Manchuria and Corea, from which the Combined Fleet derived considerable benefit, and the assistance and cooperation of the various departments of the navy, and other offices, to which are attributed the satisfactory progress of the naval operations. I beg herewith to respectfully submit to Your Majesty the proceedings of the Naval Review, and the intimation of the conclusion of our duties corresponding to Your Majesty's order.

Heihachiro Togo,
Commander-in-Chief of the
Combined Fleet.

THE ADMIRAL'S FINAL ORDER ON DISPERSAL OF THE COMBINED FLEET.

Admiral Togo, before the dispersal of the Combined Fleet, issued the following Order to the officers and men:—

The twenty months' war has now become a thing of the past, and our Combined Fleet is about to disperse. But this will not bring any change in the responsibilities of our naval men. In order to preserve for all time the fruit of the late war, and to uphold the rising prestige of the Empire, it is necessary that the navy, which in peace or war equally must stand as the country's outer bulwark, should maintain its full strength on the sea, and be ready for any emergency.

Naval strength does not merely depend on possessing ships and guns, but mainly depends on an invisible but real power, the effective power of the men who use the ships and guns. If one gun can fire a hundred shots that hit their mark every time, it is as good as a hundred guns which can each hit only once in a hundred times. Therefore in the navy, we ought to aim at being strong, apart from the strength of the material which we handle. Our recent naval victory, while it was attributable in large measure to the illustrious virtues of H. M. the Emperor, was also due to our training in ordinary times.

If we can deduce the future from the past, we must not rest at ease, even at present when the war is concluded. The life of a naval man is a never-ceasing war and whether the country is engaged in a war or not, makes no difference in his responsibilities. In war, he may display his strength, and in peace he should accumulate it. Always he is called upon to discharge his duties. For the past year and a half, we fought against wind and wave, sustained heat and cold, and engaged the enemy in life and death struggles. It was no light task, but it may be regarded as a long series of manoeuvres. It was the fortune of the naval men, who participated in the engagements, to draw manifold lessons from them. This fortune more than made up for the hardships of war. Should the navy men allow themselves to get rusty in time of peace, the warships, however majestic their appearance may be, will be like a house built on the sand, easily destroyed by the blast of any gale. We ought to guard ourselves against such slackness.

In ancient times Corea, after conquest by Japan, was under our control for four hundred years, but was lost to Japan, through the weakening of our navy. In later times, the Tokugawa Shogunate neglected the national defence, with the result that the whole Empire was panic-struck at the advent of a few American warships, and then could not prevent Russia gaining a foothold in Saghalien. In the history of the West, the British Navy, emerging victorious at the Nile and Trafalgar, not only gave England a secure position, but, as its force was subsequently maintained at the highest standard of efficiency, has succeeded up to the present in protecting the interests and extending the influence of Great Britain.

All these facts, old and new, of the East and West, are dependent to a certain degree on political exigencies, but mainly on the question whether or not the military men forget the time of war in time of peace. We, the naval men whose fortune it is to survive the war, must add the experience obtained in the war to the training of the past, and exert ourselves for the further advancement of the navy, so that we may not fall behind the times.

Only when, being ever mindful of the Imperial instructions, we have made strenuous efforts, and kept our strength and energy up to the mark, against the time of necessity, may we hope for the successful execution of our duties of protecting the country. Heaven gives the laurels of victory in war to those only who keep themselves in training in time of peace, and WIN THE BATTLE BEFORE IT IS FOUGHT. Heaven likewise takes away the crown of victory from those who soon grow satisfied with a few victories, and allow their activities to relax in time of peace. The ancient sage says "*Tighten your helmet string after a victory!*

Heihachiro Togo,
Commander-in-Chief of the Combined Fleet.